A New Introduction to
ENGLISH LITERATURE
BOOK 3

D. J. MAY *and* L. A. HILL

LONDON
OXFORD UNIVERSITY PRESS
1970

Oxford University Press, Ely House, London W.1

GLASGOW NEW YORK TORONTO MELBOURNE WELLINGTON
CAPE TOWN SALISBURY IBADAN NAIROBI DAR ES SALAAM LUSAKA ADDIS ABABA
BOMBAY CALCUTTA MADRAS KARACHI LAHORE DACCA
KUALA LUMPUR SINGAPORE HONG KONG TOKYO

SBN 19 414463 1

© in this selection, preface, introductory notes, notes, questions and word lists Oxford University Press, 1970

Printed in Great Britain by Richard Clay (The Chaucer Press) Ltd
Bungay, Suffolk

Contents

	Preface	v
	Acknowledgements	vii
1	The Emperor Releases Gulliver	1
2	Grandpa in Bed	6
3	The Legs	9
4	Romance	12
5	The Sermon on the Mount	14
6	Jim	21
7	And Wilt Thou Leave Me Thus?	24
8	The Boarding House	27
9	A Clash at School	36
10	An Explorer in the Indonesian Islands	40
11	Cupid's Arrows	43
12	Millamant and Mirabell	49
13	Satire	52
14	Women: A Chapter of Aphorisms	55
15	The Nightingale	58
16	The School for Scandal	61
17	A Letter from Lien Chi Altangi in London	66
18	The Drunkenness of Seithenyn	70
19	Claudius Visits the Sibyl	77
20	Topsy-Turvy Land	82
21	I Will Not Let Thee Go	89

	CONTENTS	
22	Why St Gregory Sent Missionaries to the English	92
23	The Talented Man	94
24	A Love-Poet	98
25	A Portrait of Dr Johnson	101
26	The Song of the Shirt	105
27	Parson Adams Has a Fight	109
28	London at War—and After	113
29	The History of a Man of Learning	117
30	One Disadvantage of Having Money	123
	Word Lists	127

Preface

This series of books is intended to provide an easy and attractive introduction to the riches of English literature. The extracts come from a wider range of sources than is usual in such books. All the great English writers are represented in typical and, it is hoped, enjoyable passages. But in addition there will be found such items as modern biographical accounts of some of the writers, extracts from letters and diaries, pieces by scientists, criticism, and songs. The series is designed to acquaint students with all kinds of interesting ways in which the English language has been used. Introductions to each piece explain the background to it and any difficult allusions in it. The questions at the end of each piece have been very carefully designed to guide the student through the piece step by step, to help him understand its meaning fully and appreciate its qualities. The extracts range in time from one of the earliest English works of literature, the Anglo-Saxon poem *Beowulf*, to many modern English novels. Virtually every important English writer has been included.

The order of the pieces has also been carefully planned. Book 1 starts with the easiest piece, Book 5 ends with the most difficult. But each book is self-contained and can be used without it being necessary to refer to the others. In each book the pieces are arranged in order of difficulty, and also offer a varied and balanced range of styles and subject-matter. The basis for judging the difficulty of each piece was as follows. Assuming a student was familiar with L. A. Hill's basic 3,275 headword vocabulary, the number of difficulties he or she would find in each piece was counted. The average number of these difficulties per 100 words in the piece as a whole indicated how easy or hard it would be for the student, and where it should come in the sequence. A few minor adjustments were made, so that pieces with a close connection should come side by side—but in all these cases the easier piece was put later in the book, not the more difficult piece brought forward.

Notes on difficult words and phrases are also provided at the end of each piece, with the relevant line-number. These explain all the words or constructions which a student could not easily understand by referring

PREFACE

to the *Advanced Learner's Dictionary of Current English*. In these notes the following abbreviations are used:

L means 'a literary way of saying'
O means 'an old-fashioned way of saying'
P means 'a poetic way of saying'
V means 'a vulgar (low-class, or not standard) way of saying'.

At the end of the book there is a complete list, for each passage, of the words in it that are outside the 3,275 headword vocabulary. Students can either look these words up before beginning each piece, or work through the list afterwards to strengthen their hold on new items in their vocabulary.

Acknowledgements

We are indebted to the following for permission to use extracts from the books mentioned:

J. M. Dent and Sons Ltd and the Trustees for the Copyrights of the late Dylan Thomas (*Portrait of the Artist as a Young Dog*); Robert Graves (*Collected Poems, 1965*); Mrs D. M. Mewton-Wood ('Romance' by W. J. Turner); Gerald Duckworth and Co. Ltd (*Cautionary Tales for Children* by Hilaire Belloc); Jonathan Cape Ltd and the Executors of the James Joyce Estate (*Dubliners*); Cassell and Co. Ltd and Robert Graves (*Goodbye to All That*); Macmillan and Co. Ltd and Mrs George Bambridge (*Plain Tales from the Hills* by Rudyard Kipling); Constable and Co. Ltd (*Treasury of English Aphorisms* by Logan Pearsall Smith); Laurence Pollinger Ltd and the Estate of the late Mrs Frieda Lawrence (*Phoenix* by D. H. Lawrence, published by William Heinemann Ltd); Methuen and Co. Ltd and Robert Graves (*I, Claudius*); The Clarendon Press (*Shorter Poems* by Robert Bridges); Hodder and Stoughton Ltd (*Dr Johnson and Company* by Robert Lynd); and Collins Publishers (*Diaries and Letters* by Harold Nicolson).

The passages from the Authorized Version of the Bible are Crown Copyright and are reproduced by permission.

1 The Emperor Releases Gulliver

Gulliver's Travels by Jonathan Swift (1667–1745) is a story that has always given pleasure both to children and to older people. It tells of the travels of Lemuel Gulliver, and the strange countries he found himself in. On the island of Lilliput, all the people were only six inches high; in the country of Brobdingnag, all the people were giants, as tall as church towers; among other places visited by Gulliver was the land of the Houyhnhnms, which was ruled by horses who were wise and good, and where the men behaved like animals. ('Houyhnhnms', which is what the horses were called, is like the sound made by a horse.)

This extract comes from the first part of the book, describing Gulliver's stay on the island of Lilliput. On the island he was called 'the Man-Mountain'. At first the people—called Lilliputians—were afraid of him, and tied him up; but after a time they decided he would not harm them, and set him free. Here we read about his release, and the conditions made by the Emperor of Lilliput. We also read about the recovery of his hat, which was as high as a Lilliputian man, and had to be dragged by five Lilliputian horses.

In *Gulliver's Travels*, Swift delights in imagining amusing situations, especially in the Lilliput section, where the Lilliputians' reactions to Gulliver are often very funny. But the book is also a satire, mocking human stupidity. Because the Lilliputians are so small, such things as their pride and their quarrels look absurd to us; but we are also meant to think that such behaviour in real people is absurd, as would be obvious to a Gulliver looking down on *us*. So the book, while amusing us, aims also to give us a larger vision of human life. Swift no doubt took a further, personal pleasure in the fancy of being so much larger than the rest of humanity.

(Another passage by Swift is to be found in Book 2.)

About two or three days before I was set at liberty, there arrived an express to inform his Majesty that some of his subjects riding near the place where I was first taken up, had seen a great black substance lying on the ground, very oddly shaped, extending its edges round as wide as his Majesty's bedchamber, and rising up in the middle as high as a man; that it was no living creature, as they at first apprehended, for it lay on the grass without motion, and some of them had walked around it several times; that by mounting upon each other's shoulders, they had got to the top, which was flat and even, and stamping upon it they found it was hollow within; that they humbly conceived it might be something belonging to the Man-Mountain; and if his Majesty pleased, they would undertake to bring it with only five horses. I presently knew what they meant, and was glad at heart to receive this intelligence. It seems upon my first reaching the shore after our shipwreck, I was in such confusion, that before I came to the place where I went to sleep, my hat, which I had fastened with a string to my head while I was rowing, and had stuck on all the time I was swimming, fell off after I came to land; the string, as I conjecture, breaking by some accident which I never observed, but thought my hat had been lost at sea. I intreated his Imperial Majesty to give orders it might be brought to me as soon as possible, describing to him the use and the nature of it: and the next day the waggoners arrived with it, but not in a very good condition; they had bored two holes in the brim, within an inch and a half of the edge, and fastened two hooks in the holes; these hooks were tied by a long cord to the harness, and thus my hat was dragged along for above half an English mile; but the ground in that country being extremely smooth and level, it received less damage than I expected.

Two days after this adventure, the Emperor having ordered that part of his army which quarters in and about his metropolis to be in readiness, took a fancy of diverting himself in a very singular manner. He desired I would stand like a Colossus, with my legs as far asunder as I conveniently could. He then commanded his General (who was an old experienced leader, and a great patron of mine) to draw up the troops in close order, and march them under me; the foot by twenty-four in a breast, and the horse by sixteen, with drums beating, colours flying, and pikes advanced.

I had sent so many memorials and petitions for my liberty, that his Majesty at length mentioned the matter, first in the cabinet, and then in a full council; where it was opposed by none, except Skyresh Bolgolam, who was pleased, without any provocation, to be my mortal enemy. But it was carried against him by the whole board, and confirmed by the Emperor. That minister was *Galbet*, or Admiral of the Realm, very much in his master's confidence, and a person well versed in affairs, but of a morose and sour complexion. However he was at length persuaded to comply; but prevailed that the articles and conditions upon which I should be set free, and to which I must swear, should be drawn up by himself. Because the reader may be curious to have some idea of the style and manner of expression peculiar to that people, as well as to know the articles upon which I recovered my liberty, I have made a translation of the whole instrument word by word, as near as I was able, which I here offer to the public.

Golbasto Momaren Evlame Gurdilo Shefin Mully Ully Gue, most mighty Emperor of Lilliput, delight and terror of the universe, whose dominions extend five thousand *blustrugs* (about twelve miles in circumference) to the extremities of the globe; monarch of all monarchs, taller than the sons of men; whose feet press down to the centre, and whose head strikes against the sun; at whose nod the princes of the earth shake their knees; pleasant as the spring, comfortable as the summer, fruitful as autumn, dreadful as winter. His most sublime Majesty proposeth to the Man-Mountain, lately arrived to our celestial dominions, the following articles, which by a solemn oath he shall be obliged to perform.

First, The Man-Mountain shall not depart from our dominions, without our licence under our great seal.

Second, He shall not presume to come into our metropolis, without our express order; at which time, the inhabitants shall have two hours' warning to keep within their doors.

Third, The said Man-Mountain shall confine his walks to our principal high roads, and not offer to walk or lie down in a meadow or field of corn.

Fourth, As he walks the said roads, he shall take the utmost care not to trample upon the bodies of any of our loving subjects, their horses, or carriages, nor take any of our subjects into his hands, without their own consent.

Fifth, If an express requires extraordinary dispatch, the Man-Mountain shall be obliged to carry in his pocket the messenger and horse a six days' journey once in every moon, and return the said messenger back (if so required) safe to our Imperial Presence.

Sixth, He shall be our ally against our enemies in the Island of Blefescu, and do his utmost to destroy their fleet, which is now preparing to invade us.

Seventh, That the said Man-Mountain shall, at his times of leisure, be aiding and assisting to our workmen, in helping to raise certain great stones, towards covering the wall of the principal park, and other our royal buildings.

Eighth, That the said Man-Mountain shall, in two moons' time, deliver in an exact survey of the circumference of our dominions by a computation of his own paces round our coast.

Lastly, That upon his solemn oath to observe all the above articles, the said Man-Mountain shall have a daily allowance of meat and drink sufficient for the support of 1,728 of our subjects, with free access to our Royal Person, and other marks of our favour. Given at our Palace at Belfaborac the twelfth day of the ninety-first moon of our reign.

JONATHAN SWIFT

NOTES

1 *set at liberty:* released.
2 *express:* urgent letter.
3 *taken up.* Gulliver was found lying asleep. The Lilliputians tied him up and carried him to their city on a big cart pulled by horses.
6 *apprehended:* thought. (O)
10 *within:* inside. (O).
13 *presently:* immediately. (O)
14 *intelligence:* news.
31 *took a fancy of diverting:* decided he would like to divert. (O)
31 *singular:* strange; unusual.
34 *draw up the troops in close order:* make the troops parade in lines, with each man close to his neighbours.
35 *the foot:* the soldiers who fight on foot; the infantry.
35 *by twenty-four in a breast:* in lines composed of twenty-four men side by side. (O)
36 *the horse:* the soldiers who fight on horseback; the cavalry.
37 *colours flying:* flags not rolled up.
37 *pikes advanced:* pikes held forward, horizontally, or nearly so.
38 *memorials:* letters containing requests.
42 *mortal enemy:* enemy for the whole of his life.
48 *drawn up:* prepared.
49 *peculiar to:* used only by.
51 *instrument:* formal document.
61 *proposeth:* proposes. (O)
69 *within their doors:* inside their houses; indoors. (O)
71 *offer:* attempt.
79 *moon:* month; twenty-eight days. (O)
85 *be aiding and assisting to:* aid and assist. (O)

86 *towards:* for the purpose of; as a help in.
87 *other our royal buildings:* other royal buildings of ours. (O)
89 *deliver in:* hand in to the proper authorities.
93 *meat:* food. (O)
95 *given:* dated.

QUESTIONS

1 Why was Gulliver's hat damaged by the men who brought it? But why was it less damaged than he had expected?
2 What did the Emperor ask Gulliver to do while the army marched with their drums and colours?
3 In what ways was Gulliver required to help the people of Lilliput, as a condition of his release?
4 The Emperor's declaration about Gulliver's release is one of the main places here where his pride is made to look absurd, because we remember how small he is. Find as many places in the declaration as you can where we might laugh at the Emperor's idea of himself.

2 Grandpa in Bed

Dylan Thomas (1914–53) was one of the most remarkable poets of recent years, and also wrote some entertaining prose works. This extract is from his book *Portrait of the Artist as a Young Dog*, which he published in 1940 when he was twenty-six. The title of the book echoes the title of another, more famous book by a modern writer, *A Portrait of the Artist as a Young Man*, by James Joyce (Piece 8 in this book is a story by him). Joyce's book (published in 1916) describes the development of a young man who is going to become a writer, and is obviously based very largely on Joyce's own experiences. Dylan Thomas's book is a similar story of a boy's development, based on his own life. But Thomas's book is more light and joking—a 'young dog' suggests someone who is gay and naughty. In this passage he remembers a visit to his 'grandpa', or grandfather. According to the writer, his grandfather used to like sitting up in bed at night imagining he was being drawn along by horses, as in a coach. With his tongue he used to imitate the sound of the horses' feet. But he did not like other people to know about it. It is an amusing but sympathetic picture of 'grandpa' that Dylan Thomas draws.

In the middle of the night I woke from a dream full of whips and lariats as long as serpents, and runaway coaches on mountain passes, and wide, windy gallops over cactus fields, and I heard the old man in the next room crying 'Gee-up!' and 'Whoa!' and trotting his tongue on the roof of his mouth.

It was the first time I had stayed in grandpa's house. The floorboards had squeaked like mice as I climbed into bed, and the mice between the walls had creaked like wood as though another visitor was walking on them. It was a mild summer night, but curtains had flapped and branches beaten against the window. I had pulled the sheets over my head, and soon was roaring and riding in a book.

'Whoa there, my beauties!' cried grandpa. His voice sounded very young and loud, and his tongue had powerful hooves, and he made his bedroom into a great meadow. I thought I would see if he was ill, or had set his bedclothes on fire, for my mother had said that he lit his pipe under the blankets, and had warned me to run to his help if I smelt smoke in the night. I went on tiptoe through the darkness to his bedroom door, brushing against the furniture and upsetting the candlestick with a thump. When I saw there was a light in the room I felt frightened, and as I opened the door I heard grandpa shout 'Gee-up!' as loudly as a bull with a megaphone.

He was sitting straight up in bed and rocking from side to side as though the bed were on a rough road; the knotted edges of the counterpane were his reins; his invisible horses stood in a shadow beside the bedside candle. Over a white flannel nightshirt he was wearing a red waistcoat with walnut-sized brass buttons. The overfilled bowl of his pipe smouldered among his whiskers like a little burning hayrick on a stick. At the sight of me, his hands dropped from the reins and lay blue and quiet, the bed stopped still on a level road, and he muffled his tongue into silence, and the horses drew softly up.

'Is there anything the matter, grandpa?' I asked, though the clothes were not on fire. His face in the candlelight looked like a ragged quilt pinned upright on the black air and patched all over with goat-beards.

He stared at me mildly. Then he blew down his pipe, scattering the sparks and making a high, wet dog-whistle of the stem, and shouted 'Ask no questions'.

After a pause, he said slyly, 'Do you ever have nightmares, boy?' I said 'No.'

'Oh, yes, you do,' he said.

I said I was woken by a voice that was shouting to horses.

'What did I tell you?' he said. 'You eat too much. Who ever heard of horses in a bedroom?'

He fumbled under his pillow, brought out a small, tinkling bag, and carefully untied its strings. He put a sovereign in my hand, and said 'Buy a cake'. I thanked him and wished him good night.

As I closed my bedroom door, I heard his voice crying loudly and gaily, 'Gee-up! gee-up!' and the rocking of the travelling bed.

DYLAN THOMAS

NOTES

4 *trotting his tongue on the roof of his mouth:* making a noise like a horse trotting, by striking his tongue against the roof of his mouth.

13 *his tongue had powerful hooves:* the noise his tongue made was like that of a horse with powerful hooves.

26 *walnut-sized:* as big as walnuts.

30 *drew softly up:* stopped gently; stopped gradually.

8 DYLAN THOMAS

QUESTIONS

1 Why do you think the writer had the dreams he describes in the first paragraph?
2 What did he do when he first got into bed?
3 When he first heard the noises coming from his grandfather's bedroom, what did he think might have happened?
4 Grandpa used to imitate the sound made by the horses' feet with his tongue. What other things did he actually *do* (and not just imagine) in order to pretend he was driving horses like a coachman?
5 In some places Dylan Thomas writes about the scene as though grandpa really was driving horses: for instance, in lines 28–9 he writes 'his hands dropped from the reins ... the bed stopped still on a level road', as though grandpa really was holding reins and the bed really was moving. Find further places in the piece where Thomas writes of the scene in this way, as though he saw it through grandpa's eyes.
6 How did grandpa explain the fact that the boy had heard noises?
7 Why do you think he gave the boy a sovereign?
8 Dylan Thomas makes his picture vivid with similes (comparisons of one thing with another) and metaphors (describing one thing as though it was another). Explain the following similes:

   a 'as loudly as a bull with a megaphone' (line 21).
   b 'like a little burning hayrick on a stick' (lines 27–8).
   c 'like a ragged quilt pinned upright on the black air and patched all over with goat-beards' (lines 32–3).

Explain also the following metaphors:

   d 'the floorboards had squeaked like mice' (lines 6–7). (This is actually a metaphor followed by a simile to help to explain it; the same is true of *e*.)
   e 'the mice ... had creaked like wood' (lines 7–8).

3 The Legs

Robert Graves is a very remarkable modern writer, who has written poetry, novels, and autobiography (books about oneself). One important idea in his work is that people should be individuals, not afraid to behave differently from other people. This poem is about the way people imitate other people, and do what is expected of them, without thinking: they are represented in the poem as legs with no heads! But Robert Graves admits how easy it is to let oneself follow the crowd.

In this book we also have an extract from Graves's account of his schooldays (page 36) and an extract from his novel *I, Claudius* (page 77), so it will be possible later to compare his ideas in these different works.

There was this road,
And it led up-hill,
And it led down-hill,
And round and in and out.

And the traffic was legs,
Legs from the knees down,
Coming and going,
Never pausing.

And the gutters gurgled
With the rain's overflow,
And the sticks on the pavement
Blindly tapped and tapped.

What drew the legs along
Was the never-stopping,
And the senseless, frightening
Fate of being legs.

Legs for the road,
The road for legs,
Resolutely nowhere
In both directions.

My legs at least
Were not in that rout:
On grass by the roadside
Entire I stood,

Watching the unstoppable
Legs go by
With never a stumble
Between step and step.

Though my smile was broad
The legs could not see,
Though my laugh was loud
The legs could not hear.

My head dizzied, then:
I wondered suddenly,
Might I too be a walker
From the knees down?

Gently I touched my shins.
The doubt unchained them:
They had run in twenty puddles
Before I regained them.

ROBERT GRAVES

NOTES

27 *with never a stumble:* never stumbling; without a single stumble. (O or P)

QUESTIONS

1 Why did the legs keep moving?
2 What does the speaker mean when he says the legs went 'resolutely nowhere' (line 19)?
3 What does the speaker mean when he says he was 'entire' (line 24)?
4 Was the speaker happy when standing by the roadside?
5 Say in your own words what happened to the speaker, as described in the last two verses of the poem.
6 Although this is a poem, the only rhymes at the end of lines are in the last verse. Find them. Do you think they are attractive or not? Why?

4 Romance

The last poem, by Robert Graves, was rather satirical; this poem, by an early twentieth-century poet called W. J. Turner, is by contrast very romantic—in fact it is called 'Romance'. It is about the way in which a boy's mind was drawn away from reality by dreams of strange lands. Chimborazo and Cotopaxi are great volcanoes in Ecuador, in South America; Popocatapetl is a volcano in Mexico. The sound of their names haunted the boy. But he was not interested in what the volcanoes, or the countries they were in, were really like. It was the 'golden dream' that the names put in his head that 'stole him away'.

> When I was but thirteen or so
>   I went into a golden land,
> Chimborazo, Cotopaxi,
>   Took me by the hand.
>
> My father died, my brother too,
>   They passed like fleeting dreams,
> I stood where Popocatapetl
>   In the sunlight gleams.
>
> I dimly heard the master's voice
>   And boys far-off at play,
> Chimborazo, Cotopaxi,
>   Had stolen me away.
>
> I walked in a great golden dream
>   The town street, to and fro—
> Shining Popocatapetl
>   Gleamed with his cap of snow.

I walked home with a gold dark boy
   And never a word I'd say,
Chimborazo, Cotopaxi,
   Had taken my breath away.   20

I gazed entranced upon his face
   Fairer than any flower—
O shining Popocatapetl,
   It was thy magic hour:

The houses, people, traffic seemed
   Thin fading dreams by day,
Chimborazo, Cotopaxi,
   They had stolen my soul away!

W. J. TURNER

NOTES

1 *thirteen or so:* about thirteen.
13 *I walked . . . the . . . street:* I walked . . . along the . . . street.
14 *to and fro:* backwards and forwards.
18 *never a word I'd say:* I wouldn't say a single word. (O or P)
22 *fairer:* more beautiful. (O)

QUESTIONS

1 Great volcanic mountains might seem frightening objects. How do we know, from the first verse of this poem, that in the boy's imagination they were friendly and inviting?
2 For the boy, the dream became reality and reality became like a dream. Find the places in the poem where reality is shown as being like a dream to him.
3 Was the 'gold dark boy' (line 17) a real boy he walked home from school with, or an invention of his imagination?
4 Why does he say (line 24) that it was Popocatapetl's 'magic hour'?
5 The poem ends 'They had stolen my soul away'. Find evidence in the poem that the boy had become unconcerned with the fate of other people.

5 The Sermon on the Mount

The Bible is the book of holy writings of the Christian Church, consisting of the Old Testament, or the holy writings of the Jews, and the New Testament, describing the life of Jesus and the deeds of his first followers, or disciples. The Old Testament was written mainly in Hebrew, the New Testament mainly in Greek; but in the early days of the Christian Church, the Bible was best known in Latin translation. The first full translation of the Bible into English was made in the fourteenth century. Other translations followed, and in 1611 what is called the 'Authorized Version' was published. This was a translation agreed on by many scholars in the Church of England, and is still the translation mostly used in England. It is in very beautiful English, and thousands of its phrases have become a common part of the English language, since in England Christians have usually been taught to read the Bible carefully.

This passage is one of the most famous in the Bible, and is given here in the 1611 Authorized Version in which English people are familiar with it. It comes from the book of the New Testament called the 'Gospel according to St Matthew', and describes how Jesus taught his disciples up on a mountainside, where he could talk to them quietly. Much of the most important teaching of Jesus is contained in this sermon: it is where he tells Christians to be humble and merciful, and if they are hit on the right cheek, not to hit back but to 'turn the other cheek'. It is impossible fully to understand English life and literature without some knowledge of the Bible, and especially of passages like this one.

And seeing the multitudes Jesus went up into a mountain: and when he was set, his disciples came unto him:

And he opened his mouth, and taught them, saying,

Blessed are the poor in spirit, for theirs is the kingdom of heaven.

Blessed are they that mourn: for they shall be comforted.

Blessed are the meek: for they shall inherit the earth.

Blessed are they which do hunger and thirst after righteousness: for they shall be filled.

Blessed are the merciful: for they shall obtain mercy.

Blessed are the pure in heart: for they shall see God.

Blessed are the peacemakers: for they shall be called the children of God.

Blessed are they which are persecuted for righteousness' sake: for theirs is the kingdom of heaven.

Blessed are ye, when men shall revile you, and persecute you, and shall say all manner of evil against you falsely, for my sake.

Rejoice, and be exceeding glad: for great is your reward in heaven: for so persecuted they the prophets which were before you.

Ye are the salt of the earth: but if the salt have lost his savour, wherewith shall it be salted? it is thenceforth good for nothing, but to be cast out, and to be trodden under foot of men.

Ye are the light of the world. A city that is set on an hill cannot be hid.

Neither do men light a candle, and put it under a bushel, but on a candlestick; and it giveth light unto all that are in the house.

Let your light so shine before men, that they may see your good works, and glorify your Father which is in heaven.

. . .

Ye have heard that it hath been said, An eye for an eye, and a tooth for a tooth:

But I say unto you, That ye resist not evil: but whosoever shall smite thee on thy right cheek, turn to him the other also.

And if any man will sue thee at the law, and take away thy coat, let him have thy cloke also.

And whosoever shall compel thee to go a mile, go with him twain.

Give to him that asketh thee, and from him that would borrow of thee turn not thou away.

Ye have heard that it hath been said, Thou shalt love thy neighbour, and hate thine enemy.

But I say unto you, Love your enemies, bless them that curse you, do good to them that hate you, and pray for them which despitefully use you, and persecute you;

That ye may be the children of your Father which is in heaven: for he maketh his sun to rise on the evil and on the good, and sendeth rain on the just and on the unjust.

For if ye love them which love you, what reward have ye? do not even the publicans the same?

And if ye salute your brethren only, what do ye more than others? do not even the publicans so?

Be ye therefore perfect, even as your Father which is in heaven is perfect.

. . .

Lay not up for yourselves treasures upon earth, where moth and rust doth corrupt, and where thieves break through and steal:

But lay up for yourselves treasures in heaven, where neither moth nor rust doth corrupt, and where thieves do not break through nor steal:

For where your treasure is, there will your heart be also.

The light of the body is the eye: if therefore thine eye be single, thy whole body shall be full of light.

But if thine eye be evil, thy whole body shall be full of darkness. If therefore the light that is in thee be darkness, how great is that darkness!

No man can serve two masters: for either he will hate the one, and love the other; or else he will hold to the one, and despise the other. Ye cannot serve God and mammon.

Therefore I say unto you, Take no thought for your life, what ye shall eat, or what ye shall drink; nor yet for your body, what ye shall put on. Is not the life more than meat, and the body than raiment?

Behold the fowls of the air: for they sow not, neither do they reap, nor gather into barns; yet your heavenly Father feedeth them. Are ye not much better than they?

Which of you by taking thought can add one cubit unto his stature?

And why take ye thought for raiment? Consider the lilies of the field, how they grow; they toil not, neither do they spin:

And yet I say unto you, That even Solomon in all his glory was not arrayed like one of these.

Wherefore, if God so clothe the grass of the field, which today is, and tomorrow is cast into the oven, shall he not much more clothe you, O ye of little faith?

Therefore take no thought, saying, What shall we eat? or, What shall we drink? or, Wherewithal shall we be clothed?

(For after all these things do the Gentiles seek:) for your heavenly Father knoweth that ye have need of all these things.

But seek ye first the kingdom of God, and his righteousness; and all these things shall be added unto you.

Take therefore no thought for the morrow: for the morrow shall take thought for the things of itself. Sufficient unto the day is the evil thereof.

. . .

Judge not, that ye be not judged.

For with what judgment ye judge, ye shall be judged: and with what measure ye mete, it shall be measured to you again.

And why beholdest thou the mote that is in thy brother's eye, but considerest not the beam that is in thine own eye?

Or how wilt thou say to thy brother, Let me pull the mote out of thine eye; and, behold, a beam is in thine own eye?

Thou hypocrite, first cast out the beam out of thine own eye; and then shalt thou see clearly to cast the mote out of thy brother's eye.

Give not that which is holy unto the dogs, neither cast ye your pearls before swine, lest they trample them under their feet, and turn again and rend you.

Ask, and it shall be given you; seek, and ye shall find; knock, and it shall be opened unto you:

For every one that asketh receiveth; and he that seeketh findeth; and to him that knocketh it shall be opened.

Or what man is there of you, whom if his son ask bread, will he give him a stone?

Or if he ask a fish, will he give him a serpent?

If ye then, being evil, know how to give good gifts unto your children, how much more shall your Father which is in heaven give good things to them that ask him?

Therefore all things whatsoever ye would that men should do to you, do ye even so to them: for this is the law and the prophets.

Enter ye in at the strait gate: for wide is the gate, and broad is the way, that leadeth to destruction, and many there be which go in thereat.

Because strait is the gate, and narrow is the way, which leadeth unto life, and few there be that find it.

Beware of false prophets, which come to you in sheep's clothing, but inwardly they are ravening wolves.

Ye shall know them by their fruits. Do men gather grapes of thorns, or figs of thistles?

Even so every good tree bringeth forth good fruit; but a corrupt tree bringeth forth evil fruit.

A good tree cannot bring forth evil fruit, neither can a corrupt tree bring forth good fruit.

Every tree that bringeth not forth good fruit is hewn down, and cast into the fire.

Wherefore by their fruits ye shall know them.

130 Not every one that saith unto me, Lord, Lord, shall enter into the kingdom of heaven; but he that doeth the will of my Father which is in heaven.

Many will say to me in that day, Lord, Lord, have we not prophesied in thy name? and in thy name have cast out devils? and in thy name done many wonderful works?

And then will I profess unto them, I never knew you: depart from me, ye that work iniquity.

Therefore whosoever heareth these sayings of mine, and doeth them, I will liken him unto a wise man, which built his house upon 140 a rock:

And the rain descended, and the floods came, and the winds blew, and beat upon that house; and it fell not: for it was founded upon a rock.

And every one that heareth these sayings of mine, and doeth them not, shall be likened unto a foolish man, which built his house upon the sand:

And the rain descended, and the floods came, and the winds blew, and beat upon that house; and it fell: and great was the fall of it.

And it came to pass, when Jesus had ended these sayings, the people 150 were astonished at his doctrine:

For he taught them as one having authority, and not as the scribes.

THE GOSPEL ACCORDING TO ST MATTHEW

NOTES

[All the words and phrases about which notes are given below are O (old-fashioned)]

2 *unto:* to.

7 *they which do hunger:* those who are hungry.

15 *ye:* you.

16 *all manner of:* all kinds of.

17 *exceeding glad:* exceedingly glad.

18 *persecuted they:* they persecuted.

19 *if the salt have:* if the salt has.

19 *his:* its.
21 *trodden under foot of men:* trodden on by people.
22 *cannot be hid:* cannot be hidden.
25 *giveth:* gives. There are many examples of the '-eth' ending in this piece. They correspond to '-s' or '-es' in modern English.
30 *resist not:* should not resist.
33 *cloke:* cloak.
43 *maketh his sun to rise:* makes his sun rise.
52 *doth corrupt:* corrupts. 'Doth' is 'does'.
57 *single:* honest.
63 *hold to:* support.
69 *fowls:* birds.
90 *that:* so that.
93 *beholdest thou:* do you behold; do you look at.
112 *would that men should do:* would like men to do.
113 *even so:* similarly; the same.
115 *many there be:* there are many.
121 *gather grapes of thorns:* gather grapes from thorn-trees.
130 *saith:* says.
136 *profess:* declare.
137 *work:* do.
149 *came to pass:* happened.

QUESTIONS

1 Explain the meaning of the following phrases:

  a 'Blessed are they which do hunger and thirst after righteousness: for they shall be filled' (lines 7–8).
  b 'Ye are the salt of the earth' (line 19).
  c 'Let your light so shine before men, that they may see your good works, and glorify your Father which is in heaven' (lines 26–7).
  d 'An eye for an eye, and a tooth for a tooth' (lines 28–9).
  e 'whosoever shall compel thee to go a mile, go with him twain' (line 34).
  f 'he maketh his sun to rise on the evil and on the good, and sendeth rain on the just and on the unjust' (lines 43–4).
  g 'where your treasure is, there will your heart be also' (line 56).
  h 'Ye cannot serve God and mammon' (line 64).
  i 'Behold the fowls of the air: for they sow not, neither do they reap, nor gather into barns; yet your heavenly Father feedeth them' (lines 69–70).
  j 'Wherefore, if God so clothe the grass of the field, which today is, and tomorrow is cast into the oven, shall he not much more clothe you, O ye of little faith?' (lines 78–80).

20 THE GOSPEL ACCORDING TO ST MATTHEW

 k 'Take therefore no thought for the morrow: for the morrow shall take thought for the things of itself' (lines 87–8).
 l 'all things whatsoever ye would that men should do to you, do ye even so to them' (lines 112–13).
 m 'by their fruits ye shall know them' (line 129).
 n 'Not every one that saith unto me, Lord, Lord, shall enter into the kingdom of heaven; but he that doeth the will of my Father which is in heaven' (lines 130–2).

2 In lines 93–6 Jesus speaks of a man who looks at the 'mote' in his brother's eye, when he has a 'beam' in his own eye. Put into simple words Jesus' meaning here.
3 In lines 138–48 Jesus tells the story of the man who built his house on a rock, and the man who built his house on the sand. Put into simple words the lesson Jesus is teaching in this story.
4 Many people today accept Jesus' teaching and many people disagree with it. It is also possible very often to agree with some of his ideas and disagree with others. Try to find several things he says here that you agree with, and several things you disagree with—though, of course, you might agree with everything or disagree with everything, in which case try to say why.

6 Jim

Children are sometimes told very frightening stories about what will happen to them if they are naughty, and this was perhaps especially common in England in the nineteenth century, for some Victorian parents were very strict. Here is a poem by an entertaining writer called Hilaire Belloc (1870–1953) which is a kind of comic imitation of such teaching. (We call a comic imitation of a style a 'parody'.) This poem comes from a book called *Cautionary Tales for Children*, published in 1907, in a period when many nineteenth-century ideas, like excessive strictness, were being rejected and laughed at. No doubt many children read the book, but it was not really for children.

'Jim' is another form of 'James'.

> There was a Boy whose name was Jim;
> His Friends were very good to him.
> They gave him Tea, and Cakes, and Jam,
> And slices of delicious Ham,
> And Chocolate with pink inside,
> And little Tricycles to ride,
> And read him Stories through and through,
> And even took him to the Zoo—
> But there it was the dreadful Fate
> Befel him, which I now relate.   10
>
> You know—at least you *ought* to know,
> For I have often told you so—
> That Children never are allowed
> To leave their Nurses in a Crowd;
> Now this was Jim's especial Foible,
> He ran away when he was able,
> And on this inauspicious day
> He slipped his hand and ran away!
> He hadn't gone a yard when—Bang!
> With open Jaws, a Lion sprang,   20
> And hungrily began to eat
> The Boy: beginning at his feet.

Now, just imagine how it feels
When first your toes and then your heels,
And then by gradual degrees,
Your shins and ankles, calves and knees,
Are slowly eaten bit by bit.
No wonder Jim detested it!
No wonder that he shouted 'Hi!'
The Honest Keeper heard his cry.
Though very fat he almost ran
To help the little gentleman.
'Ponto!' he ordered as he came
(For Ponto was the Lion's Name),
'Ponto!' he cried, with angry Frown.
'Let go, Sir! Down, Sir! Put it down!'

The Lion made a sudden Stop,
He let the Dainty Morsel drop,
And slunk reluctant to his Cage,
Snarling with Disappointed Rage.
But when he bent him over Jim,
The Honest Keeper's Eyes were dim.
The Lion having reached his Head,
The Miserable Boy was dead!
When Nurse informed his Parents, they
Were more Concerned than I can say:—
His Mother, as she dried her eyes,
Said, 'Well—it gives me no surprise,
He would not do as he was told!'
His Father, who was self-controlled,
Bade all the children round attend
To James' miserable end,
And always keep a-hold of Nurse
For fear of finding something worse.

HILAIRE BELLOC

NOTES

10 *relate:* tell.
18 *slipped his hand:* pulled his hand from his nurse's.
41 *bent him:* bent. (O)
51 *bade ... attend:* told ... to attend. (O)
53 *a-hold:* hold. (O)

QUESTIONS

1 Explain the following phrases:

  a 'dreadful Fate' (line 9).
  b 'by gradual degrees' (line 25).
  c 'Dainty Morsel' (line 38).
  d 'The Honest Keeper's Eyes were dim' (line 42). Why were they dim?

2 Part of the rather frightening humour in this poem comes from the contrast between the horrible things being described, and the calm way in which the speaker, and other characters in the poem, talk about them. For example, in the third verse the speaker describes the way Jim was eaten bit by bit, as though he were talking about something quite unimportant—for instance, making a list of things to buy when out shopping. Find all the places you can where there is this contrast.
3 Another contrast in the poem is between the horrible happenings and the politeness of the language. What are the examples of this in line 32 and line 36?
4 Some of the lines are more shocking than they appear at first, because of this calm, polite way of speaking. Why is line 43 so alarming when you think about it?
5 The rhymes in this poem are in pairs. (Pairs of rhyming lines like this are usually called 'couplets'.) The word at the end of the second line of a couplet usually gets strong emphasis from the rhyme. Why is this dramatic in the pairs 'Bang!' and 'sprang' (lines 19 and 20), 'feels' and 'heels' (lines 23 and 24), 'degrees' and 'knees' (lines 25 and 26) and 'Cage' and 'Rage' (lines 39 and 40)?
6 Do you like this rather unusual kind of humour, or not? Try to give your reasons for what you think.

7 And Wilt Thou Leave Me Thus?

Here is a sad love song, written well over four hundred years ago, but perfectly easy for us to understand today. Sir Thomas Wyatt (1503–42), its author, was a member of the court of King Henry VIII and a lover of Anne Boleyn, who became one of Henry's six wives, before her marriage. He was very attracted by the flourishing Italian poetry of his time, and introduced into England various kinds of song imitated from the Italian. Here a man complains to a woman he has loved because she is going to leave him; and he begs her to change her mind. Each verse has a very touching refrain (a passage repeated in each verse of a song or poem, usually at the end): the speaker asks the woman four times if she will leave him, each time more strongly, and always ends 'Say nay, say nay!'—'nay' being an old form of 'no'. For the sake of the rhythm, in this poem 'loved' (line 8) must be pronounced as two syllables ('lovèd') and 'pity' (line 20) with the stress on the second syllable ('pit-èe').

And wilt thou leave me thus?
Say nay, say nay, for shame,
To save thee from the blame
Of all my grief and grame;
And wilt thou leave me thus?
 Say nay, say nay!

And wilt thou leave me thus,
That hath lovèd thee so long,
In wealth and woe among?
And is thy heart so strong
As for to leave me thus?
 Say nay, say nay!

And wilt thou leave me thus,
That hath given thee my heart,
Never for to depart,
Neither for pain nor smart;
And wilt thou leave me thus?
 Say nay, say nay!

And wilt thou leave me thus
And have no more pity
On him that loveth thee?
Alas, thy cruelty!
And wilt thou leave me thus?
Say nay, say nay!

SIR THOMAS WYATT

NOTES

1 *wilt:* the form of 'will' used with 'thou'. (O)
2 *for shame:* it would be shameful not to do so.
4 *grame:* sorrow. (O)
8 *hath:* has. (O)
9 *in ... among:* among.
10 *strong:* hard. (O)
11 *as for to:* to. (O)
15 *for to:* to. (O)
16 *smart:* pain.
21 *loveth:* loves. (O)

QUESTIONS

1 What is the reason the speaker gives in the first verse why the woman should not leave him? Put it in your own words.
2 In the second and third verses the speaker uses a different argument with the woman. What is this?
3 In the last verse, at one point the speaker seems to accept that he has lost the woman. Where is this?
4 Does the poem conclude with the speaker having lost hope?
5 In most of the poem, the rhythm is what we call 'iambic' rhythm: an unstressed syllable followed by a stressed syllable, then another unstressed followed by another stressed, and so on. For example, if we mark an unstressed syllable ⌣, and a stressed /, we can indicate the rhythm of the first line as

$$\smile \;/ \quad \smile \;/ \quad \smile \;/$$
And wilt | thou leave | me thus?

Each of these pairs of syllables (⌣ /) is called an iambic foot. But in some lines an unexpected variation of this produces a dramatic effect. For instance in lines 15 and 16, the first foot is the opposite of an iambic—it consists of a stressed syllable followed by an unstressed (which we call a 'trochaic' foot).

26 SIR THOMAS WYATT

This means that each line begins rather sharply and forcefully. Line 15 has a second trochaic foot following the first.

$$\text{Néver} \mid \text{fór to} \mid \text{depárt}$$

$$\text{Néither} \mid \text{for páin} \mid \text{nor smárt}$$

Why do you think this unexpected emphasis is especially dramatic, and especially suitable, on these words at this point in the poem?

8 The Boarding House

The Irish writer James Joyce (1882–1941) was mentioned in the introduction to Passage 2 ('Grandpa in Bed') as being the author of *A Portrait of the Artist as a Young Man*. Joyce's most famous book is a later work, *Ulysses*, first published in 1922: in this very long book, he tells the story of a day in Dublin, the capital of Ireland, and by going deep into the minds of his characters, reveals the whole pattern of their lives. But his first work of fiction (a work of fiction is a work about imaginary, not real people or events), *Dubliners*, a group of short stories published in 1914, was more straightforward and true to life in manner. This is one of those stories. Although very plain in its language, it is a brilliant piece of work, since little by little it builds up a detailed, quite convincing picture of the way two young people have their future determined for them, and what they feel about it.

Mrs Mooney was a butcher's daughter. She was a woman who was quite able to keep things to herself: a determined woman. She had married her father's foreman, and opened a butcher's shop near Spring Gardens. But as soon as his father-in-law was dead Mr Mooney began to go to the devil. He drank, plundered the till, ran headlong into debt. It was no use making him take the pledge: he was sure to break out again a few days after. By fighting his wife in the presence of customers and by buying bad meat he ruined his business. One night he went for his wife with the cleaver, and she had to sleep in a neighbour's house.

After that they lived apart. She went to the priest and got a separation from him, with care of the children. She would give him neither money nor food nor house-room; and so he was obliged to enlist himself as a sheriff's man. He was a shabby stooped little drunkard with a white face and a white moustache and white eyebrows, pencilled above his little eyes, which were pink-veined and raw; and all day long he sat in the bailiff's room, waiting to be put on a job. Mrs Mooney, who had taken what remained of her money out of the butcher business and set up a boarding house in Hardwicke Street, was a big imposing woman. Her house had a floating population made up of tourists from Liverpool and the Isle of Man and, occasionally, artistes from the music halls. Its resident population was made up of clerks from the city. She governed the house cunningly and firmly, knew when to give credit, when to be stern and when to let things pass. All the resident young men spoke of her as 'The Madam'.

Mrs Mooney's young men paid fifteen shillings a week for board and lodgings (beer or stout at dinner excluded). They shared in common tastes and occupations and for this reason they were very chummy with one another. They discussed with one another the chances of favourites and outsiders. Jack Mooney, the Madam's son, who was clerk to a commission agent in Fleet Street, had the reputation of being a hard case. He was fond of using soldier's obscenities: usually he came home in the small hours. When he met his friends he had always a good one to tell them, and he was always sure to be on to a good thing—that is to say, a likely horse or a likely artiste. He was also handy with the mits and sang comic songs. On Sunday nights there would often be a reunion in Mrs Mooney's front drawing-room. The music-hall artistes would oblige; and Sheridan played waltzes and polkas and vamped accompaniments. Polly Mooney, the Madam's daughter, would also sing. She sang:

> I'm a ... naughty girl
> You needn't sham:
> You know I am.

Polly was a slim girl of nineteen; she had light soft hair and a small full mouth. Her eyes, which were grey with a shade of green through them, had a habit of glancing upwards when she spoke with anyone, which made her look like a little perverse madonna. Mrs Mooney had first sent her daughter to be a typist in a corn-factor's office, but as a disreputable sheriff's man used to come every other day to the office, asking to be allowed to say a word to his daughter, she had taken her daughter home again and set her to do housework. As Polly was very lively, the intention was to give her the run of the young men. Besides, young men like to feel that there is a young woman not very far away. Polly, of course, flirted with the young men, but Mrs Mooney, who was a shrewd judge, knew that the young men were only passing the time away: none of them meant business. Things went on so for a long time, and Mrs Mooney began to think of sending Polly back to typewriting, when she noticed that something was going on between Polly and one of the young men. She watched the pair and kept her own counsel.

Polly knew that she was being watched, but still her mother's persistent silence could not be misunderstood. There had been no open complicity between mother and daughter, no open understanding, but though people in the house began to talk of the affair, still Mrs Mooney did not intervene. Polly began to grow a little strange in her manner, and the young man was evidently perturbed. At last, when she judged it to be the right moment, Mrs Mooney intervened. She dealt with moral problems as a cleaver deals with meat: and in this she had made up her mind.

It was a bright Sunday morning of early summer, promising heat, but with a fresh breeze blowing. All the windows of the boarding house were open and the lace curtains ballooned gently towards the street beneath the raised sashes. The belfry of George's Church sent out constant peals, and worshippers, singly or in groups, traversed the little circus before the church, revealing their purpose by their self-contained demeanour no less than by the little volumes in their gloved hands. Breakfast was over in the boarding house, and the table of the breakfast-room was covered with plates on which lay yellow streaks of eggs with morsels of bacon-fat and bacon-rind. Mrs Mooney sat in the straw armchair and watched the servant Mary remove the breakfast things. She made Mary collect the crusts and pieces of broken bread to help to make Tuesday's bread-pudding. When the table was cleared, the broken bread collected, the sugar and butter safe under lock and key, she began to reconstruct the interview which she had had the night before with Polly. Things were as she had suspected: she had been frank in her questions and Polly had been frank in her answers. Both had been somewhat awkward, of course. She had been made awkward by her not wishing to receive the news in too cavalier a fashion or to seem to have connived, and Polly had been made awkward not merely because allusions of that kind always made her awkward, but also because she did not wish it to be thought that in her wise innocence she had divined the intention behind her mother's tolerance.

Mrs Mooney glanced instinctively at the little gilt clock on the mantelpiece as soon as she had become aware through her reverie that the bells of George's Church had stopped ringing. It was seventeen minutes past eleven: she would have lots of time to have the matter out with Mr Doran and then catch short twelve at Marlborough Street. She was sure she would win. To begin with, she had all the weight of social opinion on her side: she was an outraged mother. She had allowed him to live beneath her roof, assuming that he was a man of honour, and he had simply abused her hospitality. He was thirty-four or thirty-five years of age, so that youth could not be pleaded as his excuse; nor could ignorance be his excuse, since he was a man who had seen something of the world. He had simply taken advantage of Polly's youth and inexperience: that was evident. The question was: What reparation would he make?

There must be reparation made in such a case. It is all very well for the man: he can go his ways as if nothing had happened, having had his moment of pleasure, but the girl has to bear the brunt. Some mothers would be content to patch up such an affair for a sum of money: she had known cases of it. But she would not do so. For her only one reparation could make up for the loss of her daughter's honour: marriage.

She counted all her cards again before sending Mary up to Mr Doran's room to say that she wished to speak with him. She felt sure she would win. He was a serious young man, not rakish or loud-voiced like the others. If it had been Mr Sheridan or Mr Meade or Bantam Lyons, her task would have been much harder. She did not think he would face publicity. All the lodgers in the house knew something of the affair; details had been invented by some. Besides, he had been employed for thirteen years in a great Catholic wine-merchant's office, and publicity would mean for him, perhaps, the loss of his job. Whereas if he agreed all might be well. She knew he had a good screw for one thing, and she suspected he had a bit of stuff put by.

Nearly the half-hour! She stood up and surveyed herself in the pier-glass. The decisive expression of her great florid face satisfied her, and she thought of some mothers she knew who could not get their daughters off their hands.

Mr Doran was very anxious indeed this Sunday morning. He had made two attempts to shave, but his hand had been so unsteady that he had been obliged to desist. Three days' reddish beard fringed his jaws, and every two or three minutes a mist gathered on his glasses so that he had to take them off and polish them with his pocket-handkerchief. The recollection of his confession of the night before was a cause of acute pain to him; the priest had drawn out every ridiculous detail of the affair, and in the end had so magnified his sin that he was almost thankful at being afforded a loophole of reparation. The harm was done. What could he do now but marry her or run away? He could not brazen it out. The affair would be sure to be talked of, and his employer would be certain to hear of it. Dublin is such a small city: everyone knows everyone else's business. He felt his heart leap warmly in his throat as he heard in his excited imagination old Mr Leonard calling out in his rasping voice: 'Send Mr Doran here, please.'

All his long years of service gone for nothing! All his industry and diligence thrown away! As a young man he had sown his wild oats, of course; he had boasted of his free-thinking and denied the existence of God to his companions in public-houses. But that was all passed and done with . . . nearly. He still bought a copy of *Reynolds's Newspaper* every week, but he attended to his religious duties, and for nine-tenths of the year lived a regular life. He had money enough to settle down on; it was not that. But the family would look down on her. First of all there was her disreputable father, and then her mother's boarding house was beginning to get a certain fame. He had a notion that he was being had. He could imagine his friends talking of the affair and laughing. She *was* a little vulgar; sometimes she said 'I seen' and 'If I had've known'. But what would grammar matter if he really loved her? He could not make up his mind whether to like her or despise her for what she had done. Of course he had done it too. His instinct urged him to remain free, not to marry. Once you are married you are done for, it said.

While he was sitting helplessly on the side of the bed in shirt and trousers, she tapped lightly at his door and entered. She told him all, that she had made a clean breast of it to her mother and that her mother would speak with him that morning. She cried and threw her arms round his neck, saying:

'O Bob! Bob! What am I to do? What am I to do at all?'

She would put an end to herself, she said.

He comforted her feebly, telling her not to cry, that it would be all right, never fear. He felt against his shirt the agitation of her bosom.

It was not altogether his fault that it had happened. He remembered well, with the curious patient memory of the celibate, the first casual caresses her dress, her breath, her fingers had given him. Then late one night as he was undressing for bed she had tapped at his door, timidly. She wanted to relight her candle at his, for hers had been blown out by a gust. It was her bath night. She wore a loose open combing-jacket of printed flannel. Her white instep shone in the opening of her furry slippers and the blood glowed warmly behind her perfumed skin. From her hands and wrists too as she lit and steadied her candle a faint perfume arose.

On nights when he came in very late it was she who warmed up his dinner. He scarcely knew what he was eating feeling her beside him alone, at night, in the sleeping house. And her thoughtfulness! If the night was anyway cold or wet or windy there was sure to be a little tumbler of punch ready for him. Perhaps they could be happy together . . .

They used to go upstairs together on tiptoe, each with a candle, and on the third landing exchange reluctant good nights. They used to kiss. He remembered well her eyes, the touch of her hand and his delirium . . .

But delirium passes. He echoed her phrase, applying it to himself: 'What am I to do?' The instinct of the celibate warned him to hold back. But the sin was there; even his sense of honour told him that reparation must be made for such a sin.

While he was sitting with her on the side of the bed Mary came to the door and said that the missus wanted to see him in the parlour. He stood up to put on his coat and waistcoat, more helpless than ever. When he was dressed he went over to her to comfort her. It would be all right, never fear. He left her crying on the bed and moaning softly: 'O my God!'

Going down the stairs his glasses became so dimmed with moisture that he had to take them off and polish them. He longed to ascend through the roof and fly away to another country where he would never hear again of his trouble, and yet a force pushed him downstairs step by step. The implacable faces of his employer and of the Madam stared upon his discomfiture. On the last flight of stairs he passed Jack Mooney, who was coming up from the pantry nursing two bottles of Bass. They saluted coldly; and the lover's eyes rested for a second or two on a thick bulldog face and a pair of thick short arms. When he reached the foot of the staircase he glanced up and saw Jack regarding him from the door of the return-room.

Suddenly he remembered the night when one of the music-hall artistes, a little blond Londoner, had made a rather free allusion to Polly. The reunion had been almost broken up on account of Jack's violence. Everyone tried to quiet him. The music-hall artiste, a little paler than usual, kept smiling and saying that there was no harm meant; but Jack kept shouting at him that if any fellow tried that sort of a game on with his sister he'd bloody well put his teeth down his throat: so he would.

Polly sat for a little time on the side of the bed, crying. Then she dried her eyes and went over to the looking-glass. She dipped the end of the towel in the water-jug and refreshed her eyes with the cool water. She looked at herself in profile and readjusted a hairpin above her ear. Then she went back to the bed again and sat at the foot. She regarded the pillows for a long time, and the sight of them awakened in her mind secret, amiable memories. She rested the nape of her neck against the cool iron bedrail and fell into a reverie. There was no longer any perturbation visible on her face.

She waited on patiently, almost cheerfully, without alarm, her memories gradually giving place to hopes and visions of the future. Her hopes and visions were so intricate that she no longer saw the white pillows on which her gaze was fixed, or remembered that she was waiting for anything.

At last she heard her mother calling. She started to her feet and ran to the banisters.

'Polly! Polly!'

'Yes, mamma?'

'Come down, dear. Mr Doran wants to speak to you.'

Then she remembered what she had been waiting for.

JAMES JOYCE

NOTES

6 *take the pledge:* promise solemnly not to drink strong drink.
9 *went for:* attacked.
13 *house-room:* permission to live in her house.
14 *sheriff's man:* a local official, whose main duty was to seize people's property when this was ordered by the law courts.
16 *pencilled:* thin, as if drawn with a pencil.
20 *floating:* composed of people who did not stay very long; always changing.
30 *favourites:* horses which were expected to win a race.
30 *outsiders:* horses which were expected not to win a race.
32 *hard case:* a tough, badly behaved sort of person.
33 *the small hours:* after midnight.
34 *a good one:* a good joke.

34 *be on to a good thing:* have secret information, or useful secret contacts.
36 *handy with the mits:* good at boxing.
38 *oblige:* be kind enough to help.
44 *full:* with pleasantly thick lips.
52 *give her the run of:* enable her to get to know freely.
56 *meant business:* was serious.
75 *circus:* round place where roads meet.
84 *under lock and key:* locked up.
88 *cavalier:* off-hand; casual; behaving as if the matter was not serious.
92 *wise innocence:* pretending to be innocent because it is wiser to appear to be so.
97 *have the matter out:* discuss the matter thoroughly and openly.
98 *catch short twelve at Marlborough Street:* get to Marlborough Street before twelve. (O)
108 *all very well:* easy enough.
115 *counted all her cards:* went through all the points which were in her favour.
125 *screw:* salary. (V)
125 *for one thing:* firstly.
125 *stuff put by:* money saved up.
129 *get . . . off their hands:* get rid of the responsibility of having to look after.
139 *afforded:* allowed.
147 *industry:* hard work.
148 *sown his wild oats:* led the gay life of a young man before settling down to serious things.
157 *had:* cheated; tricked.
162 *done for:* finished.
166 *made a clean breast of it:* confessed it all.
179 *combing-jacket:* coat worn by a woman to protect her clothes while she is combing her hair.
187 *anyway:* at all.
209 *flight of stairs:* staircase.
210 *nursing:* holding carefully in his arms.
211 *Bass:* a kind of beer.
214 *return-room:* room off the landing at the back of the house. (O)
216 *free:* familiar; disrespectful.
220 *tried that sort of game on:* behaved like that.
221 *bloody:* this is a piece of bad language, a way of swearing at someone. (V)
230 *bedrail:* rail at the head or foot of the bed.
233 *giving place to:* being replaced by.

… THE BOARDING HOUSE 35

QUESTIONS

1 Why did Mrs Mooney get a separation from her husband?
2 What was the real reason why Mrs Mooney liked having Polly working at home?
3 What took place between Polly and the young man, Bob, before Mrs Mooney intervened?
4 Most of this story takes place on a Sunday morning. But some important things had happened the previous day. What had happened on that Saturday night:

a to Polly;
b to Bob?

5 Why does Bob feel he will have to marry Polly? Give all the reasons you can find mentioned in the story.
6 What does Bob feel about marrying Polly? What seems attractive to him in the idea of marrying her and what seems unattractive?
7 In the last part of the story (lines 223–36) the author tries to convey Polly's feelings about the idea of marrying Bob. Polly does not think things out so clearly as Bob, so the author has to hint more delicately at Polly's feelings. Put in simple words what you think Polly's main feeling is.
8 In what ways is Mrs Mooney responsible for the fact that her daughter and Bob will now (as far as we are told) get married? Is she satisfied with the marriage?
9 In lines 67–8, we are told that Mrs Mooney 'dealt with moral problems as a cleaver deals with meat'. Explain why this is an appropriate simile.
10 In small details, scattered through the story, the author gives a clear idea of the physical appearance of the characters. Go through the story, finding as many details as you can about the appearance of:

a Mrs Mooney;
b Polly;
c Bob.

9 A Clash at School

Here we have a prose piece by Robert Graves, whose poem 'The Legs' appears on page 9. This comes from his story of his early life, *Goodbye to All That*, published in 1929. It describes an incident that took place before the First World War at Charterhouse, the school Robert Graves went to. Charterhouse is one of Great Britain's well-known expensive boarding schools, that is to say schools where the pupils live in term-time.

Two terms previously, there had been a famous meeting of the school Debating Society, the committee of which consisted of sixth-form boys. Though the debates were pretty dull, what passed for intellectual life at Charterhouse was represented by the Debating Society, and *The Carthusian*, always edited by two members of this committee—both institutions being free from the control of masters. One Saturday debate-night the usual decorous conventions were broken by a riotous entry of 'bloods'—members of the cricket and football elevens. The bloods were the ruling caste at Charterhouse; the eleventh man in the football eleven, though he might be a member of the under-fourth form, enjoyed far more prestige than the most brilliant scholar in the sixth. Even 'Head of the School' was an empty title. But the sixth-form intellectuals and the bloods never fought. The bloods had nothing to gain by a clash; the intellectuals were happy to be left alone. So this invasion of the bloods, just returned from winning an 'away' match, and full of beer, caused the Debating Society a good deal of embarrassment. The bloods disturbed the meeting by cheers and cat-calls, and slammed the library magazine-folders on the table. Mansfield, as president of the society, called them to order, and when they continued the disturbance, closed the debate.

The bloods thought the incident finished, but they thought wrong. A letter appeared in *The Carthusian* a few days later, protesting against the bad behaviour in the Debating Society of 'certain First Eleven babies'. The three sets of initials signed were those of Mansfield, Waller and Taylor. The school was astonished by this suicidally daring act. The Captain of Football swore that he'd chuck the three signatories into the fountain in Founder's Court. But somehow he did not. The fact was that this happened early in the autumn term, and only two other First Eleven colours had been left over from the preceding year; new colours were given gradually as the football season advanced. The other rowdies had been merely embryo bloods. So the matter had to be settled between these three sixth-form intellectuals and the three colours of the First Eleven. But the First Eleven were uncomfortably aware that Mansfield was the heavy-weight boxing champion of the school, Waller the runner-up for the middle-weights, and that Taylor was also a tough fellow to be reckoned with. While they were wondering what on earth to do, Mansfield decided to take the war into his enemies' country.

The social code of Charterhouse rested on a strict caste system; the caste marks being slight distinctions in dress. A new boy had no privileges at all; a boy in his second term might wear a knitted tie instead of a plain one; a boy in his second year might wear coloured socks; the third year gave most of the main privileges—turned-down collars, coloured handkerchiefs, a coat with a long roll, and so on; fourth year, a few more, such as the right to get up raffles; but peculiar distinctions were observed for the bloods. These included light-grey flannel trousers, butterfly collars, jackets slit up the back, and the right of walking arm-in-arm.

So the next Sunday Mansfield, Waller and Taylor did the bravest deed ever done at Charterhouse. Chapel began at eleven in the morning, but the school had to be in its seats by five minutes to eleven and sit waiting there. At two minutes to eleven the bloods used to stalk up; at one and a half minutes to, came the masters; at one minute to, came the choir in their surplices; then the headmaster arrived, and the service began. If any boy, accidentally late, sneaked in between five minutes to, and two minutes to, the hour, six hundred pairs of eyes followed him; he heard whispering and giggling at his apparent foolhardiness in pretending to be a blood. On this Sunday, then, when the bloods had entered with their usual swaggering assurance, an extraordinary thing happened.

The three sixth-formers slowly walked up the aisle, magnificent in light-grey flannel trousers, slit jackets, butterfly collars, and each wore a pink carnation in his lapel. Astonished and horrified by the spectacle, everyone turned to gaze at the Captain of the First Eleven; he had gone quite white. But by this time the masters had entered, followed by the choir, and the opening hymn, though raggedly sung, ended the tension. When chapel emptied, it always emptied according to 'school order', that is, according to position in work: the sixth form therefore went out first. The bloods not being at all high in school order, Mansfield, Waller and Taylor had the start of them. After chapel on Sunday, the custom in the autumn term was for boys to meet and gossip in the library; so to the library Mansfield, Waller and Taylor went. On the way, they buttonholed a talkative master, drew him in with them and kept him talking until dinner-time. If the bloods had dared to do anything violent they would have had to do it at once, but to make a scene in the presence of a master was impossible. Mansfield, Waller and Taylor went down to their houses for dinner, still talking to the master. After that, they always went about together in public, and the school, particularly the lower school, which had long chafed under the dress regulations, made heroes of them and began scoffing at the bloods as weak-kneed.

Finally, the captain of the eleven complained to Rendall [the headmaster] about this breach of school conventions, asking for permission to enforce the bloods' rights by disciplinary measures. Rendall, who was a scholar and disliked the games tradition, refused his request, insisting that the sixth form deserved as distinctive privileges as the First Eleven, and were, in his opinion, entitled to hold what they had assumed. The prestige of the bloods declined greatly.

ROBERT GRAVES

NOTES

2 *sixth-form:* the highest class in a British secondary school.

3 *pretty:* rather.

3 *passed for:* was accepted as.

5 *The Carthusian:* the name of the school magazine. 'Carthusian' is the adjective of 'Charterhouse'.

8 *bloods:* young men who consider themselves very superior to their fellows.

11 *under-fourth form:* the lower division of the fourth class, which was one of the lowest classes in a public school. Boys were put into classes and moved up from class to class not according to age, but according to ability, so that it was possible for a very clever sixteen-year-old boy to be in the sixth form, and a very stupid nineteen-year-old boy in the lower fourth form.

11 *enjoyed:* had the advantage of.

16 *an 'away' match:* a match played away from their school.

19 *called them to order:* asked them to behave according to the rules of the Debating Society.

A CLASH AT SCHOOL 39

27 *Founder's Court:* the courtyard named after the founder of Charterhouse.
29 *First Eleven colours:* boys who had been made full members of the First Eleven team, and were therefore allowed to wear certain clothes which other boys were not.
31 *embryo bloods:* not yet full bloods, because they had not yet got their First Eleven colours (see line 29, above).
37 *wondering what on earth to do:* a strong way of saying 'wondering what to do'. It emphasizes how puzzled they were
44 *roll:* cloth which is rolled up.
45 *get up:* organize.
45 *peculiar:* special.

47 *butterfly collars:* collars like this:

73 *buttonholed:* started a close conversation with.
76 *make a scene:* cause trouble.

QUESTIONS

1 Explain the following phrases:
   a 'The bloods had nothing to gain by a clash' (lines 13–14).
   b 'the intellectuals were happy to be left alone' (lines 14–15).
   c 'this suicidally daring act' (lines 25–6).
   d 'take the war into his enemies' country' (lines 37–8).
   e 'slight distinctions in dress' (line 40).
   f 'their usual swaggering assurance' (lines 59–60).
   g 'had long chafed under the dress regulations' (lines 79–80).
   h 'The prestige of the bloods declined greatly' (line 88).

2 What did the 'bloods' do to anger the 'intellectuals'?
3 How did the 'intellectuals' reply?
4 Why was the action taken by Mansfield, Waller and Taylor thought by the school to be 'suicidally daring'?
5 Why did the 'bloods' do nothing to Mansfield and the other two boys?
6 What did Mansfield and the other two boys do in chapel?
7 How did they avoid the 'bloods' after chapel?
8 What did the school begin to think about the 'bloods' after this?
9 What did the headmaster decide?
10 Do you think the headmaster decided rightly?
11 In what way does this story remind you of the ideas expressed by Robert Graves in 'The Legs'?

10 An Explorer in the Indonesian Islands

Alfred Russel Wallace (1823–1913) was a nineteenth-century explorer who spent many years travelling around the islands of what is now the Republic of Indonesia. These two pieces come from his book *The Malay Archipelago* (1868). The first describes his experience in a village in the Celebes where most of the inhabitants had not seen a white man before. The second describes a remarkable fruit that grows in these tropical islands. In both pieces his very plain, direct way of writing makes them enjoyable. He likes to see the facts clearly, whether good or bad: he does not like to deceive himself, and he does not like other people to deceive themselves.

Not a single person in the village could speak more than a few words of Malay, and hardly any of the people appeared to have seen a European before. One most disagreeable result of this was that I excited terror alike in man and beast. Wherever I went, dogs barked, children screamed, women ran away, and men stared as though I were some strange and terrible cannibal monster. Even the pack-horses on the roads and paths would start aside when I appeared and rush into the jungle; and as to those horrid, ugly brutes, the buffaloes, they could never be approached by me; not for fear of my own but of others' safety. They would first stick out their necks and stare at me, and then on a nearer view break loose from their halters and tethers, and rush away helter-skelter as if a demon were after them, without any regard for what might be in their way. Whenever I met buffaloes carrying packs along a pathway, or being driven home to the village, I had to turn aside into the jungle and hide myself till they had passed, to avoid a catastrophe which would increase the dislike with which I was already regarded. Every day about noon the buffaloes were brought into the village and were tethered in the shade around the houses; and then I had to creep about like a thief by back ways, for no one could tell what mischief they might do to children and houses were I to walk among them. If I came suddenly upon a well where women were drawing water or children bathing, a sudden flight was the certain result; which things occurring day after day, were very unpleasant to a person who does not like to be disliked, and who had never been accustomed to be treated as an ogre.

. . .

The Durian grows on a large and lofty forest tree, somewhat resembling an elm, but with a more smooth and scaly bark. The fruit is round or slightly oval, and about the size of a large cocoanut, of a green colour, and covered all over with short stout spines. It is so completely armed, that if the stalk is broken off it is a difficult matter to lift one from the ground. The outer rind is so thick and tough, that from whatever height it may fall, it is never broken. Inside is an oval mass of cream-coloured pulp. This pulp is the eatable part, and its consistency and flavour are indescribable. A rich butter-like custard highly flavoured with almonds gives the best general idea of it, but intermingled with it come wafts of flavour that call to mind cream-cheese, onion-sauce, brown sherry, and other incongruities. It is neither acid, nor sweet, nor juicy, yet one feels the want of none of these qualities, for it is perfect as it is. It produces no nausea or other bad effect, and the more you eat of it, the less you feel inclined to stop. In fact to eat Durians is a new sensation, worth a voyage to the East to experience.

The Durian is, however, sometimes dangerous. When the fruit begins to ripen it falls daily and almost hourly, and accidents not infrequently happen to persons walking or working under the trees. Poets and moralists, judging from our English trees and fruits, have thought that small fruits always grew on lofty trees, so that their fall should be harmless to man, while the large ones trailed on the ground. Two of the largest and heaviest fruits known, however, the Brazil-nut fruit and the Durian, grow on lofty forest trees, from which they fall as soon as they are ripe, and often wound or kill the native inhabitants. From this we may learn two things: first, not to draw general conclusions from a very partial view of nature; and secondly, that trees and fruits, no less than the varied productions of the animal kingdom, do not appear to be organized with exclusive reference to the use and convenience of man.

ALFRED RUSSEL WALLACE

NOTES

4 *excited:* caused; aroused.
7 *start:* move suddenly because of fear.
11 *on a nearer view:* when they saw me more closely.
22 *flight:* running away.
26 *Durian:* a fruit which is described in this piece.
28 *cocoanut:* coconut. (O)
36 *call to mind:* remind one of.
38 *want:* lack. (O)

QUESTIONS

1 Why did Wallace hide in the jungle when he met buffaloes coming along a path?
2 How did he avoid the buffaloes in the village in the afternoon?
3 Why have some English poets and moralists thought that trees and their fruits were organized for the convenience of men?
4 How does the Durian tree prove that this is not so?
5 What does Wallace mean when he says that we should not 'draw general conclusions from a very partial view of nature'?
6 Describe your impressions of Wallace's character as we see it reflected in these two passages.

11 Cupid's Arrows

Here we have another piece set in the East—in India, also some time in the middle of the nineteenth century. This is a short story by Rudyard Kipling (1865–1936), a great deal of whose writing was about British India, as it was called. Like the story by James Joyce (page 27), it is about a girl whose mother wants her to get married. But this girl escapes in a very dramatic way from the unattractive marriage that has been planned for her. Notice how different Kipling's style of story-telling is from Joyce's. Joyce builds up his story from many small, exactly observed details, and the emotion he produces in us grows slowly. Kipling, on the contrary, often writes in a very exaggerated way (as when he says Barr-Saggott was 'the ugliest man in Asia, with two exceptions'). Kipling is trying to amuse us all the time, and he succeeds; but we do not get such an intimate knowledge of his characters as we do of Joyce's. This story comes from Kipling's *Plain Tales from the Hills* (1888).

Once upon a time there lived at Simla a very pretty girl, the daughter of a poor but honest District and Sessions Judge. She was a good girl, but could not help knowing her power and using it. Her Mamma was very anxious about her daughter's future, as all good Mammas should be.

When a man is a Commissioner and a bachelor, and has the right of wearing open-work jam-tart jewels in gold and enamel on his clothes, and of going through a door before every one except a Member of Council, a Lieutenant-Governor, or a Viceroy, he is worth marrying. At least, that is what ladies say. There was a Commissioner in Simla, in those days, who was, and wore and did all I have said. He was a plain man—an ugly man—the ugliest man in Asia, with two exceptions. His was a face to dream about and try to carve on a pipe-head afterwards. His name was Saggott—Barr-Saggott—Anthony Barr-Saggott and six letters to follow. Departmentally, he was one of the best men the Government of India owned. Socially, he was like unto a blandishing gorilla.

When he turned his attentions to Miss Beighton, I believe that Mrs Beighton wept with delight at the reward Providence had sent her in her old age.

Mr Beighton held his tongue. He was an easy-going man.

A Commissioner is very rich. His pay is beyond the dreams of avarice—is so enormous that he can afford to save and scrape in a way that would almost discredit a Member of Council. Most Commissioners are mean; but Barr-Saggott was an exception. He entertained royally; he horsed himself well; he gave dances; he was a power in the land; and he behaved as such.

Consider that everything I am writing of took place in an almost pre-historic era in the history of British India. Some folk may remember the years before lawn-tennis was born when we all played croquet. There were seasons before that, if you will believe me, when even croquet had not been invented, and archery—which was revived in England in 1844—was as great a pest as lawn-tennis is now. People talked learnedly about 'holding' and 'loosing', 'steles', 'reflexed bows', '56-pound bows', 'backed' or 'self-yew bows', as we talk about 'rallies', 'volleys', 'smashes', 'returns' and '16-ounce rackets'.

Miss Beighton shot divinely over ladies' distance—60 yards that is—and was acknowledged the best lady archer in Simla. Men called her 'Diana of Tara-Devi'.

Barr-Saggott paid her great attention; and, as I have said, the heart of her mother was uplifted in consequence. Kitty Beighton took matters more calmly. It was pleasant to be singled out by a Commissioner with letters after his name, and to fill the hearts of other girls with bad feelings. But there was no denying the fact that Barr-Saggott was phenomenally ugly; and all his attempts to adorn himself only made him more grotesque. He was not christened 'The Langur'—which means gray ape—for nothing. It was pleasant, Kitty thought, to have him at her feet, but it was better to escape from him and ride with the graceless Cubbon—the man in a Dragoon Regiment at Umballa—the boy with a handsome face and no prospects. Kitty liked Cubbon more than a little. He never pretended for a moment that he was anything less than head over heels in love with her; for he was an honest boy. So Kitty fled, now and again, from the stately wooings of Barr-Saggott to the company of young Cubbon, and was scolded by her Mamma in consequence. 'But, Mother,' she said, 'Mr Saggott is such—such a—is so *fearfully* ugly, you know!'

'My dear,' said Mrs Beighton piously, 'we cannot be other than an all-ruling Providence has made us. Besides you will take precedence of your own Mother, you know? Think of that and be reasonable.'

Then Kitty put up her little chin and said irreverent things about precedence, and Commissioners, and matrimony. Mr Beighton rubbed the top of his head; for he was an easy-going man.

Late in the season, when he judged that the time was ripe, Barr-Saggott developed a plan which did great credit to his administrative powers. He arranged an archery-tournament for ladies, with a most sumptuous diamond-studded bracelet as prize. He drew up his terms skilfully, and every one saw that the bracelet was a gift to Miss Beighton; the acceptance carrying with it the hand and the heart of Commissioner Barr-Saggott. The terms were a St Leonard's Round—thirty-six yards—under the rules of the Simla Toxophilite Society.

All Simla was invited. There were beautifully arranged tea-tables under the deodars at Annandale, where the Grand-Stand is now; and, alone in its glory, sat the diamond bracelet in a blue velvet case. Miss Beighton was anxious—almost too anxious—to compete. On the appointed afternoon all Simla rode down to Annandale to witness the Judgment of Paris turned upside down. Kitty rode with young Cubbon, and it was easy to see that the boy was troubled in his mind. He must be held innocent of everything that followed. Kitty was pale and nervous, and looked long at the bracelet. Barr-Saggott was gorgeously dressed, even more nervous than Kitty, and more hideous than ever.

Mrs Beighton smiled condescendingly, as befitted the mother of a potential Commissioneress, and the shooting began; all the world standing a semi-circle as the ladies came out one after the other. Nothing is so tedious as an archery competition. They shot, and they shot, and they kept on shooting, till the sun left the valley, and little breezes got up in the deodars, and people waited for Miss Beighton to shoot and win. Cubbon was at one horn of the semi-circle round the shooters, and Barr-Saggot at the other. Miss Beighton was last on the list. The scoring had been weak, and the bracelet, with Commissioner Barr-Saggott, was hers to a certainty.

The Commissioner strung her bow with his own sacred hands. She stepped forward, looked at the bracelet, and her first arrow went true to a hair—full into the heart of the 'gold'—counting nine points.

Young Cubbon on the left turned white, and his Devil prompted Barr-Saggott to smile. Now horses used to shy when Barr-Saggott smiled. Kitty saw that smile. She looked to her left-front, gave an almost imperceptible nod to Cubbon, and went on shooting.

I wish I could describe the scene that followed. It was out of the ordinary and most improper. Miss Kitty fitted her arrows with immense deliberation, so that every one might see what she was doing. She was a perfect shot; and her 46-pound bow suited her to a nicety. She pinned the wooden legs of the target with great care four successive times. She pinned the wooden top of the target once, and all the ladies looked at each other. Then she began some fancy shooting at the white, which if you hit it, counts exactly one point. She put five arrows into the white. It was wonderful archery; but, seeing that her business was to make 'golds' and win the bracelet, Barr-Saggott turned a delicate green like young water-grass. Next, she shot over the target twice, then wide to the left twice—always with the same deliberation—while a chilly hush fell over the company, and Mrs Beighton took out her handkerchief. Then Kitty shot at the ground in front of the target, and split several arrows. Then she made a red—or seven points—just to show what she could do if she liked, and she finished up her amazing performance with some more fancy shooting at the target support. Here is her score as it was pricked off:

	Gold	Red	Blue	Black	White	Total Hits	Total Score
Miss Beighton	1	1	0	0	5	7	21

Barr-Saggott looked as if the last few arrow-heads had been driven into his legs instead of the target's, and the deep stillness was broken by a little snubby, mottled, half-grown girl saying in a shrill voice of triumph, 'Then *I've* won!'

Mrs Beighton did her best to bear up; but she wept in the presence of the people. No training could help her through such a disappointment. Kitty unstrung her bow with a vicious jerk, and went back to her place, while Barr-Saggott was trying to pretend that he enjoyed snapping the bracelet on the snubby girl's raw, red wrist. It was an awkward scene—most awkward. Every one tried to depart in a body, and leave Kitty to the mercy of her Mamma.

But Cubbon took her away instead, and—the rest isn't worth printing.

RUDYARD KIPLING

CUPID'S ARROWS 47

NOTES

2 *Sessions Judge:* judge who goes round regularly from one town to another.
7 *jam-tart:* looking like little round tarts filled with jam.
13 *pipe-head:* the thick part of a pipe, in which one puts the tobacco.
15 *six letters to follow:* letters such as C.M.G. (Companion of the Most Distinguished Order of St Michael and St George).
16 *like unto:* like. (O)
17 *blandishing:* trying to be soft and gentle in order to win favour.
21 *held his tongue:* remained silent.
21 *easy-going:* informal; tolerant; preferring a quiet, easy life.
23 *scrape:* live very economically in order to save money.
24 *discredit:* make to lose all his credit or reputation.
26 *horsed himself well:* provided himself with good horses.
29 *pre-historic:* Kipling is joking here.
34–6 These are specialized terms used in archery and tennis which do not need explaining here, as their meaning has no importance to the story.
39 *Diana:* the Roman goddess of hunting.
47 *gray:* another spelling of 'grey'.
49 *graceless:* who has no sense of what is right and proper.
50 *prospects:* expectations of becoming rich or important.
52 *head over heels:* completely; madly.
58 *all-ruling:* which rules everything.
66 *diamond-studded:* studded with diamonds; set with diamonds.
66 *drew up his terms:* composed his conditions.
70 *Toxophilite:* Archery.
76 Paris was a hero in Greek myth. He had to choose who was the most beautiful of three goddesses.
83 *Commissioneress:* joking word for the wife of a Commissioner.
84 *standing a semi-circle:* standing in a semi-circle. (O)
93 *true to a hair:* absolutely straight; not a hair's breadth out of line.
94 *the 'gold':* the centre part of the target, coloured gold.
97 *left-front:* a quarter left.
116 *pricked off:* marked up by the person who was keeping the score.
122 *snubby:* having a short, turned-up nose.
122 *half-grown:* who has not yet finished growing.
124 *to bear up:* not to show her disappointment.
128 *snapping:* shutting with a snapping sound.
129 *in a body:* all together.

QUESTIONS

1 Explain the meaning of the following phrases:
   - *a* 'Socially, he was like unto a blandishing gorilla' (lines 16–17).
   - *b* 'the reward Providence had sent her in her old age' (lines 19–20).
   - *c* 'beyond the dreams of avarice' (lines 22–3).
   - *d* 'stately wooings' (line 53).
   - *e* 'you will take precedence of your own Mother' (lines 58–9).
   - *f* 'He must be held innocent of everything that followed' (line 78).
   - *g* 'the bracelet, with Commissioner Barr-Saggott, was hers to a certainty' (lines 90–1).
   - *h* 'horses used to shy when Barr-Saggott smiled' (lines 96–7). Does this remind you of Wallace in the Malay archipelago (page 40)?
   - *i* 'her business was to make "golds"' (lines 107–8).

2 What arguments did Mrs Beighton use to try to persuade Kitty to marry Mr Barr-Saggott?

3 Summarize in your own words what Kitty did to show Mr Barr-Saggott and everybody else that she did not want to marry him.

4 What do we know about Mr Beighton's character? Is it very much? Why is it appropriate that we are not told any more?

5 Who was happy at the end of the archery-tournament? Why? Who was unhappy? Why?

6 What do you think Kipling means when he says in the last sentence of the story 'the rest isn't worth printing'?

7 It has already been mentioned in the introduction to this piece that Kipling likes using amusing exaggerations. Find as many examples of this as you can.

12 Millamant and Mirabell

Now we have a passage from a play. This is by William Congreve (1670–1729), the most brilliant of a group of playwrights (writers of plays) of the later seventeenth century. This is known as the Restoration period in English history and English literature, because it was the period after the restoration of King Charles II to his throne, in 1660. (For eleven years before that, England had had no king, but had been ruled by Parliament.) King Charles and his followers had lived mainly in France before 1660, and had brought back to England with them a liking for the witty French theatre. This was no doubt one reason why so many amusing plays were written in England in this period: we call them, as a group, 'Restoration comedy'. Congreve's most famous play is *The Way of the World*, which was first performed in 1700. It is about a young man called Mirabell and a young woman called Millamant, both wealthy members of high society. Mirabell wants to marry Millamant, but she pretends to be very proud, though secretly she likes Mirabell. In this scene we see a battle of wit between them, Mirabell trying to show that women are dependent on men, and Millamant trying to show that she is quite independent of any man, and can take whatever pleasure she wants. (Witwoud, Mirabell's friend, and Fainall, Millamant's companion, are not important in this scene.)

MILLAMANT: Mirabell, did you take exceptions last night? O ay, and went away—Now I think on't I'm angry—no, now I think on't I'm pleased—for I believe I gave you some pain.

MIRABELL: Does that please you?

MILLAMANT: Infinitely; I love to give pain.

MIRABELL: You would affect a cruelty which is not in your nature; your true vanity is in the power of pleasing.

MILLAMANT: O I ask your pardon for that—one's cruelty is one's power, and when one parts with one's cruelty, one parts with one's power; and when one has parted with that, I fancy one's old and ugly.

MIRABELL: Ay, ay, suffer your cruelty to ruin the object of your power, to destroy your lover—and then how vain, how lost a thing you'll be! Nay, 'tis true: you are no longer handsome when you've lost your lover; your beauty dies upon the instant: for beauty is the lover's gift; 'tis he bestows your charms—your glass is all a cheat. The ugly and the old, whom the looking-glass mortifies, yet after commendation can be flattered by it, and discover beauties in it: for that reflects our praises, rather than your face.

MILLAMANT: O the vanity of these men! Fainall, d'ye hear him? If they did not commend us, we were not handsome! Now you must know they could not commend one, if one was not handsome. Beauty the lover's gift—Lord, what is a lover, that it can give? Why one makes lovers as fast as one pleases, and they live as long as one pleases, and they die as soon as one pleases: and then if one pleases one makes more.

WITWOUD: Very pretty. Why you make no more of making of lovers, madam, than of making so many card-matches.

MILLAMANT: One no more owes one's beauty to a lover, than one's wit to an echo: they can but reflect what we look and say; vain empty things if we are silent or unseen, and want a being.

MIRABELL: Yet, to those two vain empty things, you owe two of the greatest pleasures of your life.

MILLAMANT: How so?

MIRABELL: To your lover you owe the pleasure of hearing yourselves praised; and to an echo the pleasure of hearing yourselves talk.

WITWOUD: But I know a lady that loves talking so incessantly, she won't give an echo fair play; she has that everlasting rotation of tongue, that an echo must wait till she dies, before it can catch her last words.

MILLAMANT: O fiction; Mrs Fainall, let us leave these men.

WILLIAM CONGREVE

NOTES

1 *take exceptions:* take exception; object. (O)
2 *on't:* on it; of it. (O)
6 *affect:* pretend to have.
9 *parts with:* gets rid of.
12 *suffer:* allow.
14 *'tis:* it is. (P)
15 *upon the instant:* immediately. (O)
16 *glass:* looking-glass.
20 *d'ye:* do you. (O)
21 *were not:* would not be. (O)
28 *card-matches:* card games; competitions at playing cards.
31 *want:* lack. (O)

QUESTIONS

1 In the first lines of this passage, we learn that Millamant annoyed Mirabell the previous night, and that he went away because he was annoyed. At first, when she remembers this, Millamant is angry. Why? Then she is pleased. Why?
2 Why, according to Millamant, must women be cruel?
3 Explain what Mirabell means when he says 'you are no longer handsome when you've lost your lover ... for beauty is the lover's gift' (lines 14–16).
4 What does he mean when he says that the looking-glass 'reflects our praises, rather than your face' (line 19)?
5 Put in your own words Millamant's answer to this, 'Now you must know they could not commend one, if one was not handsome.'
6 Explain what Mirabell means when he says that women owe their two greatest pleasures to their lover, and to an echo (lines 32–3).
7 What does Witwoud mean when he says of a certain lady (no doubt he means Millamant) 'an echo must wait till she dies, before it can catch her last words' (lines 39–40)?

13 Satire

Here is another piece of writing from the Restoration period. Much of the English writing in the late seventeenth and the eighteenth centuries was satirical, and this is from a poem called *An Essay on Satire*, published in 1679. It is not certain whether this poem is by a famous poet of the time called John Dryden (1631–1700), or by a less important writer called the Earl of Mulgrave. At the time that it was published, it was believed to be by Dryden, and because a passage in it attacked a poet called the Earl of Rochester, Rochester sent some men to beat Dryden. But it is now thought to be mainly Mulgrave's work, although Dryden may have written parts of it.

The first passage we have here is a very good account of an idea common at this period: the idea that poetry is a way of pleasing and teaching at the same time. In particular, the passage tries to describe how satire works. In the second passage, the poet admits that men who write satire may be criticizing others in order to praise themselves. The 'master' referred to here (line 30) is probably Juvenal, the Roman poet of the first and second centuries, who is generally thought of as the 'father' of satire. Notice that the poem, like very much seventeenth- and eighteenth-century poetry, is in rhyming couplets (pairs of lines), with most lines consisting of five iambic feet:

How vain | a thing | is man, | and how | unwise!

We call these couplets 'heroic couplets'. With the repeated 'bang! bang!' of their rhymes, they are good for writing with emphasis.

> How dull, and how insensible a beast
> Is man, who yet would lord it o'er the rest!
> Philosophers and poets vainly strove
> In every age the lumpish mass to move:
> But those were pedants, when compared with these,
> Who know not only to instruct but please.
> Poets alone found the delightful way,
> Mysterious morals gently to convey
> In charming numbers; so that as men grew
> Pleased with their poems, they grew wiser too.
> Satire has always shone among the rest,

And is the boldest way, if not the best,
To tell men freely of their foulest faults;
To laugh at their vain deeds, and vainer thoughts.
In satire too the wise took different ways,
To each deserving its peculiar praise.
Some did all folly with just sharpness blame,
Whilst others laughed and scorned them into shame.
But of these two, the last succeeded best,
As men aim rightest when they shoot in jest.   20

How vain a thing is man, and how unwise!
E'en he, who would himself the most despise!
I, who so wise and humble seem to be,
Now my own vanity and pride can't see.
While the world's nonsense is so sharply shown,
We pull down others, but to raise our own;
That we may angels seem, we paint them elves,
And are but satires to set up ourselves.
I, who have all this while been finding fault,
E'en with my master, who first satire taught;   30
And did by that describe the task so hard,
It seems stupendous and above reward;
Now labour with unequal force to climb
That lofty hill, unreached by former time:
'Tis just that I should to the bottom fall,
Learn to write well, or not to write at all.

Either JOHN DRYDEN *or* THE EARL OF MULGRAVE

NOTES

2 *would lord it:* wants to act like a master.
2 *o'er:* over. (O)
4 *the lumpish mass to move:* to influence the stupid masses. (O or P)
8 *mysterious morals gently to convey:* to convey mysterious morals gently. (O or P)
9 *numbers:* verses; rhythms of poetry.
16 *peculiar:* particular; suitable to itself alone.
20 *rightest:* most rightly; most accurately. (O or P)

22 *e'en*: even. (P)
27 *paint them elves*: make them out to be elves.
31 *so hard, it seems*: as being so hard that it seems.
35 *'tis*: it is. (P)

QUESTIONS

1 Put lines 1 and 2 into your own words. In what way is this view of man similar to Swift's in *Gulliver's Travels* (Piece 1 in this book).
2 In lines 3 and 4, the author talks of a past time when philosophers and poets tried to make people more understanding and good. Does he say that they were successful?
3 In lines 9 and 10, the author explains how poets have now found a successful way of influencing people and making them better. Put this explanation into your own words.
4 In lines 17 and 18, the author describes two ways of telling people about their faults. What are these two ways?
5 Why is the second way more successful?
6 Explain line 27: 'That we may angels seem, we paint them elves.'
7 Explain the last two lines.

14 Women: A Chapter of Aphorisms

An 'aphorism' is a comment on some subject attractively or wittily expressed in a few words. Logan Pearsall Smith was a modern writer who in 1928 published a book called *A Treasury of English Aphorisms*, in which he collected hundreds of aphorisms on many subjects. We have here a chapter from that book: the chapter containing aphorisms about women. Most of the aphorisms are taken from the works of well-known English writers: Dr Johnson (see later, pages 98, 101 and 117); Ben Jonson, the playwright (1572–1637); Alexander Pope, the poet (1688–1744); Lord Chesterfield (1694–1773), who wrote some famous letters to his son; William Hazlitt, the essayist and journalist (1778–1830); and Edward Gibbon, the historian (1737–94). Ralph Waldo Emerson (1803–82) was an American poet and philosopher. The other people whose sayings are quoted are not so well known.

As the faculty of writing has been chiefly a masculine endowment, the reproach of making the world miserable has been always thrown upon the women.

Dr Johnson

A woman, the more curious she is about her face, is commonly the more careless about her house.

Ben Jonson

No woman ever hates a man for being in love with her; but many a woman hates a man for being a friend to her.

Pope

Nature has given women so much power that the law has very wisely given them little.

Dr Johnson

A woman's preaching is like a dog's walking on his hinder legs. It is not done well; but you are surprised to find it done at all.

Dr Johnson

Women commonly eat more sparingly, and are less curious in the choice of meat; but if once you find a woman gluttonous, expect from her very little virtue.

Dr Johnson

Women have a perpetual envy of our vices; they are less vicious than we, not from choice, but because we restrict them.

Dr Johnson

Woman's beauty, like men's wit, is generally fatal to the owners, unless directed by a judgment which seldom accompanies a great degree of either.

Chesterfield

Ladies grow handsome by looking at themselves in the glass.

Hazlitt

Women are not formed for great cares themselves, but to soothe and soften ours.

Chesterfield

As we descend into the vale of years our infirmities require some domestic female society.

Gibbon

By permitting your reflection to carry you from your society, you expose yourself to very hazardous conjectures.

Countess Dowager of Carlisle

Spell well, if you can.

Countess Dowager of Carlisle

Almost every woman described to you by a woman presents a tragic idea, and not an idea of well-being.

Emerson

A woman who is confuted is never convinced.

Churton Collins

Women are always on the defensive.
Churton Collins

What attracts us to a woman rarely binds us to her.
Churton Collins

Collected by LOGAN PEARSALL SMITH

NOTES

17 *curious:* difficult; not liking this and not liking that. (O)
18 *meat:* food. (O)
33 *descend into the vale of years:* become old.

QUESTIONS

1 In the first quotation, Dr Johnson says that women are usually blamed for making the world miserable. Why is this so, according to him?
2 Look through these quotations and see how many of those written by men are critical of women. Was Dr Johnson right, on the evidence given here?
3 What does Pope mean when he says 'many a woman hates a man for being a friend to her' (lines 8–9)?
4 When Dr Johnson says (lines 11–12) that 'Nature has given women so much power . . .', what kind of power do you think he means?
5 Explain what Chesterfield means by saying (lines 24–6) that woman's beauty is like men's wit.
6 If it is true, as Emerson says (lines 41–2), that women generally speak of the unhappiness, rather than the happiness, of other women, why do you think this is so?
7 What is the difference between 'confuted' and 'convinced' (line 44)?
8 Which of the remarks here by men express admiration of women?
9 Try to make up one or two aphorisms like this about either women or men, from your own observation and experience.

15 The Nightingale

D. H. Lawrence (1885–1930) is one of the most important modern English writers. He was mainly a novelist, and his novels include *Sons and Lovers*, *The Rainbow* and *Women in Love*. But he also wrote many short essays and articles, of which we have an example here. In most of his writing, Lawrence was trying to show that modern people have lost some of their capacity for happiness. He thought that this was because they live too much with their minds, and not enough with their bodies. He thought that men and women had lost their tenderness towards each other, and also that people did not get the joy that they could from the natural world about them: the sun and the sky, the land and its trees and flowers, birds and animals. Here he tries to communicate what he thinks is the happy sound of the nightingale's song (the nightingale is a well-known bird in Europe which sings very loudly, often at night). Many poets have called the nightingale's song a sad song; but Lawrence thinks that it is the poets who are sad, not the nightingale. There is a famous poem by John Keats (1795–1821) called 'Ode to a Nightingale', which describes the poet's sadness. Lawrence imagines the bird teasing Keats about this. Tuscany is a district in Italy where Lawrence was living when he wrote this article.

(There is an extract from Lawrence's novel *The Rainbow* in Book 2; poems by John Keats will be found in Book 1 and Book 5.)

Tuscany is full of nightingales, and in spring and summer they sing all the time, save in the middle of the night and the middle of the day. In the little, leafy woods that hang on the steep of the hill towards the streamlet, as maidenhair hangs on a rock, you hear them piping up again in the wanness of dawn, about four o'clock in the morning: 'Hello! Hello! Hello!' It is the brightest sound in the world, a nightingale piping up. Every time you hear it, you feel wonder and, it must be said, a thrill, because the sound is so bright, so glittering, it has so much power behind it.

10 'There goes the nightingale,' you say to yourself. It sounds in the half-dawn as if the stars were darting up from the little thicket and leaping away into the vast vagueness of the sky, to be hidden and gone. But the song rings on after sunrise, and each time you listen

again, startled, you wonder: 'Now *why* do they say he is a sad bird?'

He is the noisiest, most inconsiderate, most obstreperous and jaunty bird in the whole kingdom of birds. How John Keats managed to begin his 'Ode to a Nightingale' with 'My heart aches, and a drowsy numbness pains my senses', is a mystery to anybody acquainted with the actual song. You hear the nightingale silverily shouting: 'What? What? What, John? Heart aches and a drowsy numbness pains? Tra-la-la! Tri-li-lilylilylilylily!'

And why the Greeks said he, or she, was sobbing in a bush for a lost lover, again I don't know. 'Jug-jug-jug!' say the mediaeval writers, to represent the rolling of the little balls of lightning in the nightingale's throat. A wild, rich sound, richer than the eyes in a peacock's tail.

They say, with that 'Jug! jug! jug!', that she is sobbing. How they hear it is a mystery. How anyone who didn't have his ears on upside down ever heard the nightingale 'sobbing', I don't know.

Anyhow it's a male sound, a most intensely and undilutedly male sound. A pure assertion. There is not a hint nor a shadow of echo and hollow recall. Nothing at all like a hollow low bell! Nothing in the world so unforlorn.

Perhaps that is what made Keats straightway feel forlorn.

> Forlorn! the very word is like a bell
> To toll me back from thee to my sole self!

Perhaps that is the reason of it; why they all hear sobs in the bush, when the nightingale sings, while any honest-to-God listening person hears the ringing shouts of small cherubim. Perhaps because of the discrepancy.

D. H. LAWRENCE

NOTES

2 *save:* except.
3 *steep:* steep part.
39 *honest-to-God:* ordinary; plain.

QUESTIONS

1 This piece is full of phrases invented by Lawrence to try to make us feel the quality of the nightingale's song. Explain the following phrases:

   a 'the sound is so bright, so glittering' (line 8). What kind of objects normally glitter? (Here, of course, 'glitter' is a metaphor, like several of the expressions in the following phrases.)
   b 'It sounds in the half-dawn as if the stars were darting up from the little thicket and leaping away into the vast vagueness of the sky' (lines 10–12).
   c 'silverily shouting' (line 20).
   d 'the rolling of the little balls of lightning in the nightingale's throat' (lines 25–6).
   e 'A wild, rich sound, richer than the eyes in a peacock's tail' (lines 26–7).
   f 'A pure assertion' (line 32).
   g 'the ringing shouts of small cherubim' (line 40).

2 Why do you think Lawrence says the nightingale is 'inconsiderate' (line 16)?
3 Why does he imagine the nightingale saying 'Heart aches and a drowsy numbness pains?' (line 21)?
4 What does Lawrence mean by 'anyone who didn't have his ears on upside down' (lines 29–30)?
5 What reason does Lawrence give in the last paragraph for the fact that the poets 'hear sobs in the bush, when the nightingale sings'? What is the 'discrepancy' he speaks of in the last sentence?

16 The School for Scandal

Now we have some extracts from a play, *The School for Scandal*, written by Richard Brinsley Sheridan (1751–1816) in 1777. This is one of the best eighteenth-century comedies. In the passages we have here, we get an amusing picture of the relationship between the kind old Sir Peter Teazle, and his young wife, Lady Teazle. When Lady Teazle married Sir Peter, she was a simple girl living in the country; but in the six months during which she has been living with him in London, she has become a fashionable lady. She has also become one of the friends of Lady Sneerwell, whose greatest pleasure is in criticizing other people and in spreading unkind stories about them (it is she and her group of friends who are called 'the school for scandal'). Rowley is a friend of Sir Peter's; Snake works for Lady Sneerwell.

Sir Peter Teazle's house.
Enter Sir Peter.

SIR PETER: When an old bachelor marries a young wife, what is he to expect? 'Tis now six months since Lady Teazle made me the happiest of men—and I have been the most miserable dog ever since! We tifted a little going to church, and fairly quarrelled before the bells had done ringing. I was more than once nearly choked with gall during the honeymoon, and had lost all comfort in life before my friends had done wishing me joy. Yet I chose with caution—a girl bred wholly in the country, who never knew luxury beyond one silk gown, nor dissipation above the annual gala of a race ball. Yet now she plays her part in all the extravagant fopperies of the fashion and the town, with as ready a grace as if she had never seen a bush or a grass-plot out of Grosvenor Square! I am sneered at by all my acquaintance, and paragraphed in the newspapers. She dissipates my fortune, and contradicts all my humours; yet, the worst of it is, I doubt I love her, or I should never bear all this. However, I'll never be weak enough to own it.

Enter Rowley.

ROWLEY: Oh! Sir Peter, your servant: how is it with you, sir?
SIR PETER: Very bad, Master Rowley, very bad. I meet with nothing but crosses and vexations.

ROWLEY: What can have happened to trouble you since yesterday?
SIR PETER: A good question to a married man!
ROWLEY: Nay, I'm sure your lady, Sir Peter, can't be the cause of your uneasiness.
SIR PETER: Why, has anybody told you she was dead?
ROWLEY: Come, come, Sir Peter, you love her, notwithstanding your tempers don't exactly agree.
SIR PETER: But the fault is entirely hers, Master Rowley. I am, myself, the sweetest-tempered man alive, and hate a teazing temper; and so I tell her a hundred times a day!
ROWLEY: Indeed!
SIR PETER: Aye; and what is very extraordinary, in all our disputes she is always in the wrong! But Lady Sneerwell, and the set she meets at her house, encourage the perverseness of her disposition.

Lady Sneerwell's house.
LADY SNEERWELL: The paragraphs, you say, Mr Snake, were all inserted?
SNAKE: They were, madam; and as I copied them myself in a feigned hand, there can be no suspicion whence they came.
LADY SNEERWELL: Did you circulate the report of Lady Brittle's intrigue with Captain Boastall?
SNAKE: That's in as fine a train as your ladyship could wish. In the common course of things, I think it must reach Mrs Clackitt's ears within four and twenty hours; and then, you know, the business is as good as done.
LADY SNEERWELL: Why, truly, Mrs Clackitt has a very pretty talent, and a great deal of industry.
SNAKE: True, madam, and has been tolerably successful in her day. To my knowledge she has been the cause of six matches being broken off, and three sons disinherited; of four forced elopements and as many close confinements; nine separate maintenances, and two divorces. Nay, I have more than once traced her causing a *tête-à-tête* in the *Town and Country Magazine*, when the parties, perhaps, had never seen each other's face before in the course of their lives.
LADY SNEERWELL: She certainly has talents, but her manner is gross.
SNAKE: 'Tis very true. She generally designs well, has a free tongue and a bold invention; but her colouring is too dark and her outlines

often extravagant. She wants that delicacy of tint, and mellowness of sneer, which distinguishes your ladyship's scandal.

LADY SNEERWELL: You are partial, Snake.

SNAKE: Not in the least—everybody allows that Lady Sneerwell can do more with a word or a look than many can with the most laboured detail, even when they happen to have a little truth on their side to support it.

LADY SNEERWELL: Yes, my dear Snake; and I am no hypocrite to deny the satisfaction I reap from the success of my efforts. Wounded myself in the early part of my life by the envenomed tongue of slander, I confess I have since known no pleasure equal to reducing others to the level of my own injured reputation.

Sir Peter's house.
Enter Sir Peter and Lady Teazle.

SIR PETER: Lady Teazle, Lady Teazle, I'll not bear it!

LADY TEAZLE: Sir Peter, Sir Peter, you may bear it or not, as you please; but I ought to have my own way in everything, and what's more I will, too. What! though I was educated in the country, I know very well that women of fashion in London are accountable to nobody after they are married. Why will you endeavour to make yourself so disagreeable to me, and thwart me in every little elegant expense?

SIR PETER: 'Slife, madam, I say, had you any of these little elegant expenses when you married me?

LADY TEAZLE: Lud, Sir Peter! would you have me to be out of the fashion?

SIR PETER: The fashion, indeed! what had you to do with the fashion before you married me?

LADY TEAZLE: For my part, I should think you would like to have your wife thought a woman of taste.

SIR PETER: Aye—there again—taste—Zounds! madam, you had no taste when you married me!

LADY TEAZLE: That's very true indeed, Sir Peter; and after having married you, I should never pretend to taste again, I allow. But now, Sir Peter, if we have finished our daily jangle, I presume I may go to my engagement at Lady Sneerwell's.

SIR PETER: Aye, there's another precious circumstance—a charming set of acquaintance you have made there.

LADY TEAZLE: Nay, Sir Peter, they are all people of rank and fortune, and remarkably tenacious of reputation.

SIR PETER: Yes, egad, they are tenacious of reputation with a vengeance; for they don't choose anybody should have a character but themselves! Such a crew! Ah! many a wretch has rid on a hurdle who has done less mischief than these utterers of forged tales, coiners of scandal, and clippers of reputation.

LADY TEAZLE: What! would you restrain the freedom of speech?

SIR PETER: Oh! They have made you just as bad as any one of the society.

LADY TEAZLE: Why, I believe I do bear a part with a tolerable grace. But I vow I bear no malice against the people I abuse. When I say an ill-natured thing, 'tis out of pure good humour; and I take it for granted, they deal in exactly the same manner with me. But, Sir Peter, you know you promised to come to Lady Sneerwell's too.

SIR PETER: Well, well, I'll call in just to look after my own character.

LADY TEAZLE: Then indeed you must make haste after me, or you'll be too late. So, goodbye to ye.

Exit Lady Teazle.

SIR PETER: So—I have gained much by my intended expostulation: yet with what a charming air she contradicts everything I say, and how pleasingly she shows her contempt for my authority! Well, though I can't make her love me, there is great satisfaction in quarrelling with her; and I think she never appears to such advantage as when she is doing everything in her power to plague me.

Exit.

RICHARD BRINSLEY SHERIDAN

NOTES

4 *'tis:* it is. (P)
6 *tifted:* quarrelled slightly. (O)
15 *acquaintance:* acquaintances. (O)
15 *paragraphed:* written about in social paragraphs.
16 *contradicts all my humours:* goes against whatever I feel like doing. (O)
17 *doubt:* guess.
18 *own:* admit.
22 *crosses:* irritations; things that go against one's wishes. (O)
31 *teazing:* teasing. (O)

44 *in as fine a train:* going as well.
50 *in her day:* when she was at her most successful.
51 *matches:* plans for men and women to marry.
61 *wants:* lacks. (O)
63 *you are partial:* you are biased in my favour; you show me too much favour.
83 *'Slife:* on God's life. Sir Peter is swearing. (O)
85 *Lud:* Lord; God. Lady Teazle is swearing now. (O)
91 *Zounds:* by God's (i.e. Christ's) wounds. Sir Peter is swearing again. (O)
95 *jangle:* noisy argument.
101 *egad:* by God. (O)
103 *rid:* ridden. (O)
103 *rid on a hurdle:* been carried around publicly on a hurdle as a punishment.
106 *would you:* do you want to. (O)

QUESTIONS

1 What does Sir Peter mean when he says ' 'Tis now six months since Lady Teazle made me the happiest of men—and I have been the most miserable dog ever since!' (lines 4–6)?
2 Why, according to his opening speech here, will he not tell his wife that he loves her?
3 What does Sir Peter mean when he says, in answer to Rowley, 'A good question to a married man!' (line 24)?
4 When Rowley says he is sure that Lady Teazle cannot be the cause of Sir Peter's uneasiness, why does Sir Peter reply 'Why, has anybody told you she was dead?' (line 27)?
5 What do we learn about Mrs Clackitt from the conversation between Lady Sneerwell and Snake?
6 Why, according to herself, does Lady Sneerwell enjoy spreading scandal about other people?
7 What does Lady Teazle mean when she says 'I know very well that women of fashion in London are accountable to nobody after they are married' (lines 79–80)?
8 What does Sir Peter mean (lines 91–2) when he says 'madam, you had no taste when you married me!'? And what does Lady Teazle pretend that he means when she answers 'That's very true'?
9 Why, according to herself, does Lady Teazle say ill-natured things about other people?
10 What does Sir Peter mean when he says he will call in at Lady Sneerwell's to look after his own character (line 114)?
11 Why does Lady Teazle reply that he must make haste after her or he will be too late?
12 Does Sir Peter like it when his wife contradicts him?

17 A Letter from Lien Chi Altangi in London

We have seen that the seventeenth and eighteenth centuries were a great age of satire. One good way that was used to make readers laugh at human folly was found in the passage from Swift (page 1): the life of the Lilliputians is shown there through the wondering eyes of a stranger, in this case a man who is a giant compared to them. A similar trick is used by Oliver Goldsmith (1730–74) in the passage we come to now. It is from a book called *The Citizen of the World* (1762) which consists of imaginary letters written from London to Peking by a Chinese visitor. Just as Gulliver could look with a fresh and critical eye at behaviour that the Lilliputians thought normal, so the Chinese visitor, Lien Chi Altangi, looks at the people of London. Here Lien Chi Altangi tells a comic story of the way in which frightening news grows and grows as it passes from one person to another. But we need not suppose that life in eighteenth-century England was always exactly like this!

Indulgent Nature seems to have exempted this island from many of those epidemic evils which are so fatal in other parts of the world. A want of rain but for a few days beyond the expected season in China, spreads famine, desolation, and terror, over the whole country; the winds that blow from the brown bosom of the western desert are impregnated with death in every gale; but in this fortunate land of Britain, the inhabitant courts health in every breeze, and the husbandman ever sows in joyful expectation.

But though the nation be exempt from real evils, think not, my friend, that it is more happy on this account than others. The people are afflicted, it is true, with neither famine nor pestilence, but then there is a disorder peculiar to the country, which every season makes strange ravages among them; it spreads with pestilential rapidity, and infects almost every rank of people; what is still more strange, the natives have no name for this peculiar malady, though well known to foreign physicians by the appellation of *epidemic terror*.

A season is never known to pass in which the people are not visited by this cruel calamity in one shape or another, seemingly different, though ever the same; one year it issues from a baker's shop in the shape of a sixpenny loaf, the next it takes the appearance of a comet with a fiery tail, a third it threatens like a flat-bottomed boat, and a fourth it carries consternation in the bite of a mad dog.

A dread of mad dogs is the *epidemic terror* which now prevails, and the whole nation is at present actually groaning under the malignity of its influence. The terror at first feebly enters with a disregarded story of a little dog, that had gone through a neighbouring village, that was thought to be mad by several that had seen him. The next account comes, that a mastiff ran through a certain town, and had bit five geese, which immediately ran mad, foamed at the bill, and died in great agonies soon after. Then comes an affecting history of a little boy bit in the leg, and gone down to be dipt in the salt water; when the people have sufficiently shuddered at that, they are the next congealed with a frightful account of a man who was said lately to have died from a bite he had received some years before. This relation only prepares the way for another, still more hideous, as how the master of a family, with seven small children, were all bit by a mad lap dog, and how the poor father first perceived the infection by calling for a draught of water, where he saw the lap dog swimming in the cup.

When epidemic terror is thus once excited, every morning comes loaded with some new disaster; as in stories of ghosts each loves to hear the account, though it only serves to make him uneasy, so here each listens with eagerness, and adds to the tidings with new circumstances of peculiar horror. A lady for instance, in the country, of very weak nerves has been frighted by the barking of a dog; and this, alas! too frequently happens. The story soon is improved and spreads, that a mad dog had frighted a lady of distinction. These circumstances begin to grow terrible before they have reached the neighbouring village, and there the report is that a lady of quality was *bit* by a mad mastiff. This account every moment gathers new strength and grows more dismal as it approaches the capital, and by the time it has arrived in town the lady is described, with wild eyes, foaming mouth, running mad upon all four, barking like a dog, biting her servants, and at last smothered between two beds by the advice of her doctors: while the mad mastiff is in the meantime ranging the whole country over, slavering at the mouth, and seeking whom he may devour.

My landlady, a good-natured woman, but a little credulous, waked me some mornings ago before the usual hour with horror and astonishment in her looks. She desired me if I had any regard for my safety, to keep within; for a few days ago so dismal an accident had happened, as to put all the world upon their guard. A mad dog in the country, she assured me, had bit a farmer, who soon becoming mad ran into his own yard, and bit a fine brindled cow; the cow quickly became mad as the man, began to foam at the mouth, and raising herself up, walked about on her hind legs, sometimes barking like a dog, and sometimes attempting to talk like the farmer. Upon examining the grounds of this story, I found my landlady had it from one neighbour, who had it from another neighbour, who heard it from very good authority.

Were most stories of this nature well examined, it would be found that numbers of such as have been said to suffer were no way injured, and that of those who have been actually bitten, not one in a hundred was bit by a mad dog. Such accounts in general therefore only serve to make the people miserable by false terrors, and sometimes fright the patient into actual frenzy, by creating those very symptoms they pretended to deplore.

OLIVER GOLDSMITH

NOTES

3 *want:* lack. (O)
8 *ever:* always. (O)
9 *be:* is, or may be. (O)
9 *think not:* do not think. (O)
12 *disorder:* disease.
12 *peculiar to the country:* from which only this country suffers.
28 *bit:* bitten. (O)
29 *bill:* beak.
31 *dipt:* dipped. It was believed that this was a cure if one was bitten by a mad animal. (O)
32 *the next:* next; the next moment.
34 *relation:* story.
35 *as how:* about how; as to how. (O)
37 *lap dog:* small dog which could sit on a person's lap.
45 *frighted:* frightened. (O)
49 *a lady of quality:* a lady of high position in society.
53 *upon all four:* upon all fours; on hands and knees. (O)
55 *the whole country over:* over the whole country.
60 *within:* indoors. (O)
71 *no way:* not at all; in no way. (O)
73 *serve to make:* have the effect of making.

QUESTIONS

1 Explain the following phrases:
   a 'the winds that blow from the brown bosom of the western desert are impregnated with death in every gale' (lines 4–6).
   b 'the inhabitant courts health in every breeze, and the husbandman ever sows in joyful expectation' (lines 7–8).
   c 'with pestilential rapidity' (line 13).
   d 'seemingly different, though ever the same' (lines 18–19).
   e 'The terror at first feebly enters' (line 25).
   f 'foamed at the bill' (line 29).
   g 'each loves to hear the account, though it only serves to make him uneasy' (lines 41–2).
   h 'a good-natured woman, but a little credulous' (line 57).
   i 'by creating those very symptoms they pretended to deplore' (lines 75–6).

2 Put in simple words what the writer means by 'epidemic terror'.
3 The fourth paragraph of this passage (lines 23–39) begins with the first of a number of stories each more exaggerated than the previous one. What is the first story here, out of which all the others described in the paragraph grow?
4 Put in your own words the final story of the series described in this fourth paragraph.
5 In the fifth paragraph (lines 40–56), we get a similar series of stories about a dog told by people, beginning with something quite ordinary and ending with something quite terrifying. What is the important change between the *first* and the *second* stories about a dog mentioned in this paragraph?
6 Tell in simple language the story Lien Chi Altangi's landlady told him, as described in the sixth paragraph (lines 57–69).
7 Do you think Lien Chi Altangi means it when he says (lines 68–9) that the neighbour 'heard it from very good authority'? If not, why does he say this?

18 The Drunkenness of Seithenyn

Here is a passage that combines a romantic picture of the past with some good comedy. It is from a novel called *The Misfortunes of Elphin*, published in 1829 by Thomas Love Peacock (1785–1866). Peacock was a friend of several of the Romantic poets, especially Shelley. But he was rather scornful of the Romantic tendency to make the ancient past of Britain seem like a wonderful dream. The Romantic writers had especially liked to portray in this way the Britain of Celtic times; that is to say the period before the Anglo-Saxons conquered Britain, during part of which time the legendary King Arthur was the British king. So Peacock invented his own story of those times, as a parody, or comic imitation, of the Romantic stories.

In this passage the young Prince Elphin, the king's son, is visiting another prince who lives by the sea. This prince, Seithenyn, has the duty of seeing that the embankment, which prevents the sea from flooding the land, is kept in good condition. But he prefers to spend his time drinking wine. And he gives Elphin many reasons why it is better to do nothing about the embankment. He is lazy, but he is full of clever arguments, and this makes him a very comic character. *The Misfortunes of Elphin* was also meant, in part, as a political satire on Peacock's own times; and, from this point of view, Seithenyn's arguments are to be taken as a parody of the arguments of conservative Englishmen (those who disliked change) at the beginning of the nineteenth century. Just as Seithenyn would rather see the embankment go rotten than do anything about repairing it, so—according to Peacock—the English conservatives would rather let Parliament become useless than make it more democratic and more suitable to the country's needs. The humorous and satirical note is the strongest note in this passage, but there is also a slight, pleasant Romantic feeling in it—because every successful parody has in it something of the good qualities of the work it is laughing at.

The sun had sunk beneath the waves when they reached the castle of Seithenyn. The sound of the harp and the song saluted them as they approached it. As they entered the great hall, which was already blazing with torchlight, they found his highness, and his highness's household, convincing themselves and each other with wine and wassail, of the excellence of their system of virtual superintendence; and a jovial chorus broke on the ears of the visitors.

Elphin and Teithrin stood some time on the floor of the hall before they attracted the attention of Seithenyn, who, during the chorus, was tossing and flourishing his golden goblet. The chorus had scarcely ended when he noticed them, and immediately roared aloud, 'You are welcome all four.'

Elphin answered, 'We thank you: we are but two.'

'Two or four,' said Seithenyn, 'all is one. You are welcome all. When a stranger enters, the custom in other places is to begin by washing their feet. My custom is, to begin by washing his throat. Seithenyn ap Seithyn Saidi bids you welcome.'

Elphin, taking his wine-cup, answered, 'Elphin ap Gwythno Garanhir thanks you.'

Seithenyn started up. He endeavoured to straighten himself into perpendicularity, and to stand steadily on his legs. He accomplished half his object by stiffening all his joints but those of his ankles, and from these the rest of his body vibrated upwards with the inflexibility of a bar. After thus oscillating for a time, like an inverted pendulum, finding that the attention requisite to preserve his rigidity absorbed all he could collect of his dissipated energies, and that he required a portion of them for the management of his voice, which he felt a dizzy desire to wield with peculiar steadiness in the presence of the son of the king, he suddenly relaxed the muscles that perform the operation of sitting, and dropped into his chair like a plummet. He then, with a gracious gesticulation, invited Prince Elphin to take his seat on his right hand, and proceeded to compose himself into a dignified attitude, throwing his body back into the left corner of his chair, resting his left elbow on its arm and his left cheekbone on the middle of the back of his left hand, placing his left foot on a footstool, and stretching out his right leg as straight and as far as his position allowed. He had thus his right hand at liberty, for the ornament of his eloquence and the conduct of his liquor.

Elphin seated himself at the right hand of Seithenyn. Teithrin remained at the end of the hall: on which Seithenyn exclaimed, 'Come on, man, come on. What, if you be not the son of a king, you are the guest of Seithenyn ap Seithyn Saidi. The most honourable place to the most honourable guest, and the next most honourable place to the next most honourable guest; the least honourable guest above the most honourable inmate; and, where there are but two guests, be the most honourable who he may, the least honourable of the two is next in honour to the most honourable of the two, because there are no more but two; and where there are only two, there can be nothing between. Therefore sit, and drink.'

Elphin motioned Teithrin to approach, and sit next to him.

Prince Seithenyn, whose liquor was his eating and his drinking solely, seemed to measure the gastronomy of his guests by his own; but his groom of the pantry thought the strangers might be disposed to eat, and placed before them a choice of provision, on which Teithrin ap Tathral did vigorous execution.

'I pray your excuses,' said Seithenyn, 'my stomach is weak, and I am subject to dizziness in the head, and my memory is not so good as it was, and my faculties of attention are somewhat impaired, and I would dilate more upon the topic, whereby you should hold me excused, but I am troubled with a feverishness and parching of the mouth, that very much injures my speech, and impedes my saying all I would say, and will say before I have done, in token of my loyalty and fealty to your highness and your highness's house. I must just moisten my lips, and I will then proceed with my observations. Cupbearer, fill.'

'Prince Seithenyn,' said Elphin, 'I have visited you on a subject of deep moment. Reports have been brought to me that the embankment, which has been so long entrusted to your care, is in a state of dangerous decay.'

'Decay,' said Seithenyn, 'is one thing, and danger is another. Everything that is old must decay. That the embankment is old, I am free to confess; that it is somewhat rotten in parts, I will not altogether deny; that it is any worse for that, I do most sturdily gainsay. It does its business well: it works well: it keeps out the water from the land, and it lets in the wine upon the High Commission of Embankment. Cupbearer, fill. Our ancestors were wiser than we: they built it in their wisdom; and, if we should be so rash as to try to mend it, we should only mar it.'

'The stonework,' said Teithrin, 'is sapped and mined; the piles are rotten, broken and dislocated: the floodgates and sluices are leaky and creaky.'

'That is the beauty of it,' said Seithenyn, 'Some parts of it are rotten, and some parts of it are sound.'

'It is well,' said Elphin, 'that some parts are sound: it were better that all were so.'

'So I have heard some people say before,' said Seithenyn; 'perverse people, blind to venerable antiquity: that very unamiable sort of people, who are in the habit of indulging their reason. But I say, the parts that are rotten give elasticity to those that are sound: they give them elasticity, elasticity, elasticity. If it were all sound, it would break by its own obstinate stiffness: the soundness is checked by the rottenness, and the stiffness is balanced by the elasticity. There is nothing so dangerous as innovation. See the waves in the equinoctial storms, dashing and clashing, roaring and pouring, spattering and battering, rattling and battling against it. I would not be so presumptuous as to say, I could build anything that would stand against them half an hour; and here this immortal work has stood for centuries, and will stand for centuries more, if we let it alone. It is well: it works well: let well alone. Cupbearer, fill. It was half rotten when I was born, and that is a conclusive reason why it should be three parts rotten when I die.'

The whole body of the High Commission roared approbation.

'And, after all,' said Seithenyn, 'the worst that could happen would be the overflow of a spring tide, for that was the worst that happened before the embankment was thought of; and, if the high water should come in, as it did before, the low water would go out again, as it did before, we should be no deeper in it than our ancestors were, and we could mend as easily as they could make.'

'The level of the sea,' said Teithrin, 'is materially altered.'

'The level of the sea!' exclaimed Seithenyn. 'Who ever heard of such a thing as altering the level of the sea? Alter the level of that bowl of wine before you, in which, as I sit here, I see a very ugly reflection of your very good-looking face. Alter the level of that: drink up the reflection: let me see the face without the reflection, and leave the sea to level itself.'

'Not to level the embankment,' said Teithrin.

'Good, very good,' said Seithenyn. 'I love a smart saying, though it hits at me. But, whether yours is a smart saying or no, I do not very clearly see: and, whether it hits at me or no, I do not very sensibly feel. But all is one. Cupbearer, fill.

'I think,' pursued Seithenyn, looking as intently as he could at Teithrin ap Tathral, 'I have seen something very like you before. There was a fellow here the other day very like you: he stayed here some time: he would not talk: he did nothing but drink: he used to drink till he could not stand, and then he went walking about the embankment. I suppose he thought it wanted mending; but he did not say anything. If he had, I should have told him to embank his own throat, to keep the liquor out of that. That would have posed him: he could not have answered that: he would not have a word to say for himself after that.'

'He must have been a miraculous person,' said Teithrin, 'to walk when he could not stand.'

'All is one for that,' said Seithenyn. 'Cupbearer, fill.'

'Prince Seithenyn,' said Elphin, 'if I were not aware that wine speaks in the silence of reason, I should be astonished at your strange vindication of your neglect of duty, which I take shame to myself for not having sooner known and remedied. The wise bard has well observed, "Nothing is done without the eye of the king."'

'I am very sorry,' said Seithenyn, 'that you see things in a wrong light: but we will not quarrel for three reasons: first, because you are the son of the king, and may do and say what you please, without anyone having a right to be displeased: second, because I never quarrel with a guest, even if he grows riotous in his cups: third, because there is nothing to quarrel about; and perhaps that is the best reason of the three; or rather the first is the best, because you are the son of the king; and the third is the second, that is, the second best, because there is nothing to quarrel about; and the second is nothing to the purpose, because, though guests will grow riotous in their cups, in spite of my good orderly example, God forbid I should say, that is the case with you. And I completely agree in the truth of your remark, that reason speaks in the silence of wine.'

Seithenyn accompanied his speech with a vehement swinging of his right hand: in so doing, at this point, he dropped his cup: a sudden impulse of rash volition, to pick it dexterously up before he resumed his discourse, ruined all his devices for maintaining dignity; in stooping forward from his chair, he lost his balance, and fell prostrate on the floor.

The whole body of the High Commission arose in simultaneous confusion, each zealous to be the foremost in uplifting his fallen chief. In the vehemence of their uprise, they hurled the benches backward and the tables forward; the crash of the cups and bowls accompanied their overthrow; and rivulets of liquor ran gurgling through the hall. The household wished to redeem the credit of their leader in the eyes of the Prince; but the only service they could render him was to participate in his discomfiture; for Seithenyn, as he was first in dignity, was also, as was fitting, hardest in skull; and that which had impaired his equilibrium had utterly destroyed theirs. Some fell, in the first impulse, with the tables and benches; others were tripped up by the rolling bowls; and the remainder fell at different points of progression, by jostling against each other, or stumbling over those who had fallen before them.   THOMAS LOVE PEACOCK

NOTES

10 *flourishing:* waving about.
41 *be:* are. (O)
45 *be . . . who he may:* whoever he may be.
53 *be disposed:* want.
54 *on which . . . did . . . execution:* which . . . dealt with . . .
56 *pray your excuses:* beg you to excuse me.
57 *subject to:* liable to.
59 *hold me:* consider me to be.
62 *would:* want to. (O)
67 *moment:* importance.
79 *mined:* undermined; made weak by the washing away of the earth supporting it.
79 *piles:* supporting posts.
83 *sound:* in good condition; not rotten or damaged.
84 *were . . . were:* would be . . . should be. (O)
118 *sensibly:* sensitively.
120 *pursued:* continued.
126 *embank:* build an embankment in.
127 *posed him:* set him a really difficult problem. (O)
132 *all is one for that:* that does not matter. (O)
142 *in his cups:* when he is drunk.
157 *uplifting:* lifting up; raising. (O)
158 *uprise:* standing up. (O)

QUESTIONS

1 How did Prince Seithenyn and his household convince themselves that their system of superintending the embankment was an excellent one?
2 Why do you think Seithenyn greeted Elphin and Teithrin with the cry 'You are welcome all four' (lines 11–12)?
3 If you are in class, let one or more students imitate the movements of Seithenyn described in lines 20–38.
4 Explain what is meant by saying that Seithenyn's 'liquor was his eating and drinking solely' and that he 'seemed to measure the gastronomy of his guests by his own' (lines 51–2).
5 What does Seithenyn mean when he says about the embankment 'if we should be so rash as to try to mend it, we should only mar it' (lines 77–8)?
6 List all the other arguments you can find Seithenyn giving for doing nothing about the condition of the embankment.
7 What does Teithrin mean when he says (line 108) 'The level of the sea

is materially altered', and what does Seithenyn mean when he says (lines 110–11) 'Alter the level of that bowl of wine before you'?
8 When Seithenyn tells how someone came to inspect the embankment (in fact he is right in thinking it was Teithrin) he tries to show that the man's report was not to be trusted. How does he do this (lines 120–9)?
9 What is the inconsistency in this account that Teithrin points out in reply?
10 What is the meaning of Elphin's remark 'wine speaks in the silence of reason' (lines 133–4)?
11 How does Seithenyn alter this remark of Elphin's? And why does he prefer his own version of the remark?
12 Say briefly what happens to Seithenyn and his household at the end of this passage.

19 Claudius Visits the Sibyl

In Passages 3 and 9 in this book, we have had in turn a poem by Robert Graves and an extract from his autobiography. Here we have an extract from his novel *I, Claudius* (1934). This is the story of the early life of the Roman emperor Claudius, who was born in the year 10 B.C. (before Christ) and died in A.D. (*anno Domini*—Latin for 'in the year of our Lord') 54. The story is told as if it had been written by Claudius himself, and it is a striking picture of the life of those distant times. This passage comes from the beginning of the book, where Claudius remembers how he paid a visit to the Sibyl at Cumae, a place on the Italian coast near Naples. A Sibyl was a woman through whom the gods were supposed to speak, and from whom it was thus possible to learn something of the future. This Sibyl was supposed to be inspired by Apollo, the Greek sun-god and the god of art and prophecy. (When Claudius says that some Sibyls sound as though they are inspired by Bacchus, he is referring to the fact that Bacchus was the god of wine.) At the time Claudius visited the Sibyl he was not yet emperor. In fact the mysterious prophecy that in

> Ten years, fifty days and three,
> Clau— Clau— Clau— shall given be
> A gift that all desire but he,

meant that in ten years and fifty-three days he would become emperor. It was an honour he did not want; he would have preferred to go on living quietly, writing history, which was what he had done all his life so far. Robert Graves told the story of Claudius's years as emperor in a second novel, *Claudius the God*.

I went to Cumae, in Campania, a little less than eighteen months ago, and visited the Sibyl in her cliff cavern on Mount Gaurus. There is always a Sibyl at Cumae, for when one dies her novice-attendant succeeds; but they are not all equally famous. Some of them are never granted a prophecy by Apollo in all the long years of their service. Others prophesy, indeed, but seem more inspired by Bacchus than by Apollo, the drunken nonsense they deliver; which has brought the oracle into discredit.

It was cold December weather. The cavern was a terrifying place, hollowed out from the solid rock; the approach steep, tortuous, pitch-dark, and full of bats. I went disguised but the Sibyl knew me.

It must have been my stammer that betrayed me. I stammered badly as a child and though, by following the advice of specialists in elocution, I gradually learned to control my speech on set public occasions, yet on private and unpremeditated ones I am still, though less so than formerly, liable every now and then to trip nervously over my own tongue; which is what happened to me at Cumae.

I came into the inner cavern, after groping painfully on all-fours up the stairs, and saw the Sibyl, more like an ape than a woman, sitting on a chair in a cage that hung from the ceiling, her robes red and her unblinking eyes shining red in the single red shaft of light that struck down from somewhere above. Her toothless mouth was grinning. There was a smell of death about me. But I managed to force out the salutation that I had prepared. She gave me no answer. It was only some time afterwards that I learned this was the mummied body of Deiphobe, the previous Sibyl, who had died recently at the age of 110; her eyelids were propped up with glass marbles silvered behind to make them shine. The reigning Sibyl always lived with her predecessor. Well, I must have stood for some minutes in front of Deiphobe, shivering and making propitiatory grimaces—it seemed a lifetime. At last the living Sibyl, whose name was Amalthea, quite a young woman too, revealed herself. The red shaft of light failed, so that Deiphobe disappeared—somebody, probably the novice, had covered up the tiny red-glass window—and a new shaft, white, struck down and lit up Amalthea, seated on an ivory throne in the shadows behind. She had a beautiful mad-looking face with a high forehead and sat as motionless as Deiphobe. But her eyes were closed. My knees shook and I fell into a stammer from which I could not extricate myself.

'O Sib— Sib— Sib— Sib— Sib—' I began. She opened her eyes, frowned, and mimicked me: 'O Clau— Clau— Clau—'. That shamed me and I managed to remember what I had come to ask. I said with a great effort: 'O Sibyl: I have come to question you about Rome's fate and mine.'

Gradually her face changed, the prophetic power overcame her, she struggled and gasped, and there was a rushing noise through all the galleries, doors banged, wings swished my face, the light vanished, and she uttered a Greek verse in the voice of the God:

> Who groans beneath the Punic Curse
> And strangles in the strings of purse,
> Before she mends must sicken worse.

> Her living mouth shall breed blue flies,
> And maggots creep about her eyes.
> No man shall mark the day she dies.

Then she tossed her arms over her head and began again:

> Ten years, fifty days and three,
> Clau— Clau— Clau— shall given be
> A gift that all desire but he.
>
> To a fawning fellowship
> He shall stammer, cluck, and trip,
> Dribbling always with his lip.
>
> But when he is dumb and no more here,
> Nineteen hundred years or near,
> Clau— Clau— Claudius shall speak clear.

The God laughed through her mouth then, a lovely yet terrible sound—ho! ho! ho! I made obeisance, turned hurriedly and went stumbling away, sprawling headlong down the first flight of broken stairs, cutting my forehead and knees, and so painfully out, the tremendous laughter pursuing me.

Speaking now as a practised diviner, a professional historian and a priest who has had opportunities of studying the Sibylline books as regularized by Augustus, I can interpret the verses with some confidence. By the Punic (or Carthaginian) Curse the Sibyl was referring plainly enough to the destruction of Carthage by us Romans. We have long been under a divine curse because of that. We swore friendship and protection to Carthage in the name of our principal Gods, Apollo included, and then, jealous of her quick recovery from the disasters of the Second Punic War, we tricked her into fighting the Third Punic War and utterly destroyed her, massacring her inhabitants and sowing her fields with salt. 'The strings of purse' are the chief instruments of this curse—a money-madness that has choked Rome ever since she destroyed her chief trade rival and made herself mistress of all the riches of the Mediterranean. With riches came sloth, greed, cruelty, dishonesty, cowardice, effeminacy, and every other un-Roman vice. What the gift was that all desired but myself—and it came exactly ten years and fifty-three days later—you shall read in due course. The lines about Claudius speaking clear puzzled me for years, but at last I think that I understand them. They are, I believe, an injunction to write the present work. When it is written, I shall treat it with a preservative fluid, seal it in a lead casket, and bury it deep in the ground somewhere for posterity to dig up and read. If my interpretation be correct it will be found again some 1,900 years hence. And then, when all other authors of today whose works survive will seem to shuffle and stammer, since they have written only for today, and guardedly, my story will speak out clearly and boldly.

ROBERT GRAVES

NOTES

4 *succeeds:* takes her place.
7 *...Apollo, the...:* ...Apollo, when one considers the...
7 *deliver:* speak.
14 *set:* formal.
18 *on all-fours:* on hands and knees.
25 *mummied:* mummified; prevented from decaying by use of chemicals. (L)
49 *the strings of purse:* the strings of a purse; the grip of money.
50 *mends:* gets well; gets better.
53 *mark:* notice; pay attention to.
56 *given be:* be given. (O or P)
63 *clear:* clearly.
66 *flight of ... stairs:* staircase.
67 *so painfully out:* in this way went painfully out.
70 *Sibylline:* the adjective of 'Sibyl'.
91 *be:* is. (O)

QUESTIONS

1 Explain the following phrases:

   a 'which has brought the oracle into discredit' (lines 7–8).
   b 'I am still ... liable ... to trip nervously over my tongue' (lines 15–17).
   c 'jealous of her quick recovery' (line 76).
   d 'an injunction to write the present work' (lines 87–8).
   e 'will seem to shuffle and stammer' (lines 92–3).

2 Where was Deiphobe, the former, mummified Sibyl, seated?
3 Where was Amalthea, the living Sibyl, seated?

CLAUDIUS VISITS THE SIBYL 81

4 Explain what the Sibyl meant by
   a 'the Punic Curse' (line 48).
   b 'strangles in the strings of purse' (line 49).
   c 'No man shall mark the day she dies' (line 53).
   d 'To a fawning fellowship
      He shall stammer, cluck, and trip' (lines 58–9.)
      (Notice that Claudius discusses some of these points in lines 69–86).

5 How does the Sibyl's prophecy about what will happen in 1,900 years make Robert Graves's novel seem more realistic?

20 Topsy-Turvy Land

Erewhon, published in 1872, by Samuel Butler (1835–1902), is the story of a man's visit to a remote land called 'Erewhon'—which is almost the same as 'Nowhere' spelt backwards. In Erewhon everything is done in a different way from what we are used to. The most important difference is that people who are ill are punished, and that people who commit crimes are shown sympathy and are sent for treatment or to hospital! As we read about these happenings, we are sometimes shocked, but also sometimes think how wise the Erewhonians (inhabitants of Erewhon) are. What Butler is trying to do is to make us realize how confused our own behaviour often is. We often blame and punish people for doing things that they cannot avoid doing: for instance, there is no doubt that people who commit certain crimes are often as much in need of help and kindness as people who are physically ill. But at the same time we frequently allow people to do things that harm other people, without trying to prevent them at all. Butler wants to amuse us—and to make us think about all these questions again.

(There is an extract from a letter by Samuel Butler in Book 1.)

This is what I gathered. That in that country if a man falls into ill health, or catches any disorder, or fails bodily in any way before he is seventy years old, he is tried before a jury of his countrymen, and if convicted is held up to public scorn and sentenced more or less severely as the case may be. There are subdivisions of illnesses into crimes and misdemeanours as with offences among ourselves—a man being punished very heavily for serious illness, while failure of eyes or hearing in one over sixty-five, who has had good health hitherto, is dealt with by fine only, or imprisonment in default of payment. But if a man forges a cheque, or sets his house on fire, or robs with violence from the person, or does any other such things as are criminal in our own country, he is either taken to a hospital and most carefully tended at the public expense, or if he is in good circumstances, he lets it be known to all his friends that he is suffering from a severe fit of immorality, just as we do when we are ill, and they come and visit him with great solicitude, and inquire with interest how it all came about, what symptoms first showed themselves, and so forth—questions which he will answer with great unreserve; for bad conduct, though considered no less deplorable than illness with ourselves, and as unquestionably indicating something seriously wrong with the individual who misbehaves, is nevertheless held to be the result of either pre-natal or post-natal misfortune.

During my confinement in prison, and on my journey, I had already discovered a great deal of the above; but it still seemed surpassingly strange, and I was in constant fear of committing some piece of rudeness, through my inability to look at things from the same standpoint as my neighbours; but after a few weeks' stay with the Nosnibors, I got to understand things better, especially on having heard all about my host's illness, of which he told me fully and repeatedly.

It seemed that he had been on the Stock Exchange of the city for many years and had amassed enormous wealth, without exceeding the limits of what was generally considered justifiable, or at any rate, permissible dealing; but at length on several occasions he had become aware of a desire to make money by fraudulent representations, and had actually dealt with two or three sums in a way which had made him rather uncomfortable. He had unfortunately made light of it and pooh-poohed the ailment, until circumstances eventually presented themselves which enabled him to cheat upon a very considerable scale; he told me what they were, and they were about as bad as anything could be, but I need not detail them; he seized the opportunity, and became aware, when it was too late, that he must be seriously out of order. He had neglected himself too long.

He drove home at once, broke the news to his wife and daughters as gently as he could, and sent off for one of the most celebrated straighteners of the kingdom to a consultation with the family practitioner, for the case was plainly serious. On the arrival of the straightener he told his story, and expressed his fear that his morals must be permanently impaired.

The eminent man reassured him with a few cheering words, and then proceeded to make a more careful diagnosis of the case. He inquired concerning Mr Nosnibor's parents—had their moral health been good? He was answered that there had not been anything seriously amiss with them, but that his maternal grandfather, whom he was supposed to resemble somewhat in person, had been a consummate scoundrel and had ended his days in a hospital—while a brother of his father's, after having led a most flagitious life for many years, had been at last cured by a philosopher of a new school, which as far as I could understand it bore much the same relation to the old as homeopathy to allopathy. The straightener shook his head at this, and laughingly replied that the cure must have been due to nature. After a few more questions he wrote a prescription and departed.

I saw the prescription. It ordered a fine to the State of double the money embezzled; no food but bread and milk for six months, and a severe flogging once a month for twelve. I was surprised to see that no part of the fine was to be paid to the poor woman whose money had been embezzled, but on inquiry I learned that she would have been prosecuted in the Misplaced Confidence Court, if she had not escaped its clutches by dying shortly after she had discovered her loss.

As for Mr Nosnibor, he had received his eleventh flogging on the day of my arrival. I saw him later on the same afternoon, and he was still twinged; but there had been no escape from following out the straightener's prescription, for the so-called sanitary laws of Erewhon are very rigorous, and unless the straightener was satisfied that his orders had been obeyed, the patient would have been taken to a hospital (as the poor are) and would have been much worse off. Such at least is the law, but it is never necessary to enforce it.

On a subsequent occasion I was present at an interview between Mr Nosnibor and the family straightener, who was considered competent to watch the completion of the cure. I was struck with the delicacy with which he avoided even the remotest semblance of inquiry after the physical well-being of his patient, though there was a certain yellowness about my host's eyes which argued a bilious habit of body. To have taken notice of this would have been a gross breach of professional etiquette. I was told, however, that a straightener sometimes thinks it right to glance at the possibility of some slight physical disorder if he finds it important in order to assist him in his diagnosis; but the answers which he gets are generally untrue or evasive, and he forms his own conclusions upon the matter as well as he can. Sensible men have been known to say that the straightener should in strict confidence be told of every physical ailment that is likely to bear upon the case; but people are naturally shy of doing this, for they do not like lowering themselves in the opinion of the straightener, and his ignorance of medical science is supreme. I heard of one lady, indeed, who had the hardihood to confess that a furious outbreak of ill-humour and extravagant fancies for which she was seeking advice was possibly the result of indisposition. 'You should resist that,' said the straightener, in a kind, but grave voice; 'we can do nothing for the bodies of our patients; such matters are beyond our province, and I desire that I may hear no further particulars.' The lady burst into tears, and promised faithfully that she would never be unwell again.

But to return to Mr Nosnibor. As the afternoon wore on many carriages drove up with callers to inquire how he had stood his flogging. It had been very severe, but the kind inquiries upon every side gave him great pleasure, and he assured me that he felt almost tempted to do wrong again by the solicitude with which his friends had treated him during his recovery; in this I need hardly say that he was not serious.

During the remainder of my stay in the country Mr Nosnibor was constantly attentive to his business, and largely increased his already great possessions; but I never heard a whisper to the effect of his having been indisposed a second time, or made money by other than the most strictly honourable means. I did hear afterwards in confidence that there had been reason to believe that his health had been not a little affected by the straightener's treatment, but his friends did not choose to be over-curious upon the subject, and on his return to his affairs it was by common consent passed over as hardly criminal in one who was otherwise so much afflicted. For they regarded bodily ailments as the more venial in proportion as they have been produced by causes independent of the constitution. Thus if a person ruin his health by excessive indulgence at the table or by drinking, they count it to be almost a part of the mental disease which brought it about, and so it goes for little; but they have no mercy on such illnesses as fevers or catarrhs or lung diseases, which to us appear to be beyond the control of the individual. They are only more lenient towards the diseases of the young—such as measles, which they think to be like sowing one's wild oats—and look over them as pardonable indiscretions if they have not been too serious, and if they are atoned for by complete subsequent recovery.

It is hardly necessary to say that the office of straightener is one which requires long and special training. It stands to reason that he who would cure a moral ailment must be practically acquainted with it in all its bearings. The student for the profession of straightener is required to set apart certain seasons for the practice of each vice in turn, as a religious duty. These seasons are called 'fasts', and are continued by the student until he finds that he really can subdue all the more usual vices in his own person, and hence can advise his patients from the results of his own experience.

Those who intend to be specialists, rather than general practitioners, devote themselves more particularly to the branch in which their practice will mainly lie. Some students have been obliged to continue their exercises during their whole lives, and some devoted men have actually died as martyrs to the drink, or gluttony, or whatever branch of vice they may have chosen for their especial study. The greater number, however, take no harm by the excursions into the various departments of vice which it is incumbent upon them to study.

For the Erewhonians hold that unalloyed virtue is not a thing to be immoderately indulged in. I was shown more than one case in which the real or supposed virtues of parents were visited upon the children to the third and fourth generation. The straighteners say that the most that can be truly said for virtue is that there is a considerable balance in its favour, and that it is on the whole a good deal better to be on its side than against it; but they urge that there is much pseudo-virtue going about, which is apt to let people in very badly before they find it out. Those men, they say, are best who are not remarkable either for vice or virtue. I told them about Hogarth's idle and industrious apprentices, but they did not seem to think that the industrious apprentice was a very nice person.

SAMUEL BUTLER

NOTES

1 *gathered:* understood.
2 *disorder:* illness.
12 *tended:* looked after.
21 *held:* considered.
37 *made light of it:* treated it as unimportant.
44 *broke the news:* announced something which till then had been a secret.
46 *straighteners:* people who straighten problems out.
58 *of a new school:* who followed new theories and methods.
59 *bore much the same relation:* was related in more or less the same way.
72 *twinged:* suffering twinges of pain.
80 *struck with:* impressed by.
83 *argued:* suggested.
92 *bear upon:* have any connection with.
103 *wore on:* went slowly on.
104 *stood:* endured; got on with.

112 *to the effect of his having:* which said that he had.
114 *in confidence:* secretly.
117 *over-curious:* too curious.
123 *brought it about:* caused it.
124 *goes for little:* is not considered important.
128 *sowing one's wild oats:* enjoying oneself while one is young, before settling down to the serious life of an adult.
128 *look over:* overlook; forgive.
131 *office:* job.
132 *stands to reason:* is only reasonable.
133 *would:* wants to. (O)
148 *hold:* think; consider.
150 *the ... virtues ... were visited upon the children:* the children suffered for the ... virtues.
155 *let people in:* let people down; disappoint people. (O)

QUESTIONS

1 Explain the following phrases:

  a 'There are subdivisions of illnesses into crimes and misdemeanours' (lines 5–6).
  b 'held to be the result of either pre-natal or post-natal misfortune' (lines 21–2).
  c 'my inability to look at things from the same standpoint as my neighbours' (lines 26–7).
  d 'a desire to make money by fraudulent representations' (line 35).
  e 'expressed his fear that his morals must be permanently impaired' (lines 48–9).
  f 'a gross breach of professional etiquette' (lines 84–5).
  g 'he felt almost tempted to do wrong again by the solicitude with which his friends had treated him during his recovery' (lines 106–8).
  h 'to set apart certain seasons for the practice of each vice in turn' (lines 135–6).
  i 'there is much pseudo-virtue going about' (lines 154–5).

2 Go through the piece noting where people in Erewhon show sympathy to their fellow-citizens who have immoral or criminal desires.

3 Mr Nosnibor gets a prescription from the 'straightener' after his 'fit of immorality'. But is the 'prescription' similar to what we would call medical treatment? If not, what is it like? What is the *main* difference between the Erewhonian treatment of crime, and ours?

4 Look at Mr Nosnibor's name carefully. What has it in common with the name 'Erewhon'?

5 Butler tells us that the 'straighteners' who deal with moral and mental disorders know nothing at all about their patients' bodies (lines 98–100). Butler no doubt intends us to turn this statement upside down and read it as a comment on our doctors: in this case, what is he saying that doctors are ignorant of?

6 What is your opinion of the Erewhonian practice of treating diseases beyond the control of the individual more severely than those that can be controlled (lines 119–26)?

7 What was the Erewhonian opinion of virtue? Do you agree or disagree with it?

21 I Will Not Let Thee Go

Here is a sentimental but pleasant poem written by Robert Bridges (1844–1930). The speaker has had a love affair with a girl which has lasted for a month, and now she says that she wants to bring it to an end. How serious she is about this we do not know—perhaps she is not very serious, and can easily be persuaded by the speaker not to leave him. He declares that he will not let her go, and each verse gives a reason why. Some of the reasons seem good ones, some are just charming and fanciful inventions. What is most important is his determination—and perhaps that will persuade her not to leave him!

> I will not let thee go.
> Ends all our month-long love in this?
>   Can it be summed up so,
>   Quit in a single kiss?
>   I will not let thee go.
>
>   I will not let thee go.
> If thy words' breath could scare thy deeds,
>   As the soft south can blow
>   And toss the feathered seeds,
>   Then might I let thee go.
>
>   I will not let thee go.
> Had not the great sun seen, I might;
>   Or were he reckoned slow
>   To bring the false to light,
>   Then might I let thee go.
>
>   I will not let thee go.
> The stars that crowd the summer skies
>   Have watched us so below
>   With all their million eyes,
>   I dare not let thee go.

> I will not let thee go.
> Have we not chid the changeful moon,
> Now rising late, and now
> Because she set too soon,
> And shall I let thee go?
>
> I will not let thee go.
> Have not the young flowers been content,
> Plucked ere their buds could blow,
> To seal our sacrament?
> I cannot let thee go.
>
> I will not let thee go.
> I hold thee by too many bands:
> Thou sayest farewell, and lo!
> I have thee by the hands,
> And will not let thee go.

ROBERT BRIDGES

NOTES

- 2 *ends all our month-long love:* does all our month-long love end. (P)
- 4 *quit:* finished. (O)
- 8 *south:* south wind. (O)
- 10 *might I:* I might. (O or P)
- 28 *blow:* open into flowers. (O or P)
- 29 *seal our sacrament:* witness and approve the holy bond between us.

QUESTIONS

1 What does the speaker refer to when he says 'this' in line 2?
2 What does he mean in Verse 2, when he says that he might let her go if the breath of her words could 'scare' her deeds? What are the 'deeds' he speaks of here? And why cannot her words 'scare' or drive her deeds away?
3 Why do you think he says in Verse 3 that he might let her go if the sun had not seen them? Does this seem to you a good reason?
4 Why does he say, later in Verse 3, that he might let her go if the sun did not show up what was true and what was false? What is it that is true that he thinks the sun has shown him?

5 What do you think he might mean in Verse 5?
6 Why (line 22) have they 'chid the changeful moon'? Why did they want the moon not to rise late and not to set too soon?
7 How (line 29) have the flowers sealed their sacrament? Do you think (line 27) that the flowers were 'content' to do this?
8 How (according to the last verse) does he physically prevent her from going?
9 Notice the variations in the last line of each verse. Why do you think the last lines of the first and last verses repeat (or almost repeat) the first line of each verse?

22 Why St Gregory Sent Missionaries to the English

Now we go back to one of the earliest incidents in English history, and one of the earliest books in the English language. The Venerable Bede was a monk who lived in the north of England early in the eighth century, soon after the Anglo-Saxons came to Britain. He wrote a history in Latin called *The Ecclesiastical History of the English Nation*. Over a hundred years later King Alfred (849–901), who was the king of the West Saxons (a part of the English people), had an English translation made of Bede's history. This passage is in a modernized form of that English. It is one of the most famous passages in the book, and tells a traditional story of why the great Roman pope, St Gregory (pope from 590 to 604), sent Christian missionaries to England.

Nor is the account of St Gregory, which has been handed down to us by the tradition of our ancestors, to be passed by in silence, in relation to his motives for taking such interest in the salvation of our nation. It is reported, that some merchants, having just arrived at Rome on a certain day, exposed many things for sale in the market-place, and abundance of people resorted thither to buy: Gregory himself went with the rest, and, among other things, some boys were set to sale, their bodies white, their countenances beautiful, and their hair very fine. Having viewed them, he asked, as is said, from what country or nation they were brought? and was told, from the island of Britain, whose inhabitants were of such personal appearance. He again inquired whether those islanders were Christians, or still involved in the errors of paganism? and was informed that they were pagans. Then fetching a deep sigh from the bottom of his heart, 'Alas! what pity,' said he, 'that the author of darkness is possessed of men of such fair countenances; and that being remarkable for such graceful aspects, their minds should be void of inward grace.' He therefore again asked, what was the name of that nation? and was answered, that they were called Angles. 'Right,' said he, 'for they have an Angelic face, and it becomes such to be co-heirs with the Angels in heaven. What is the name,' proceeded he, 'of the province from which they are brought?' It was replied, that the natives of that province were called Deiri. 'Truly they are *De Ira*,' said he, 'withdrawn from wrath, and called to the mercy of Christ. How is the king of that province called?' They told him his name was Alla: and he, alluding to the name, said, 'Hallelujah, the praise of God the Creator must be sung in those parts.'

Then repairing to the bishop of the Roman apostolical see (for he was not himself then made pope), he entreated him to send some ministers of the word into Britain to the nation of the English, by whom it might be converted to Christ; declaring himself ready to undertake that work, by the assistance of God, if the apostolic pope should think fit to have it so done. Which not being then able to perform, because, though the pope was willing to grant his request, yet the citizens of Rome could not be brought to consent that so noble, so renowned, and so learned a man should depart the city; as soon as he was himself made pope, he perfected the long-desired work, sending other preachers, but himself by his prayers and exhortations assisting the preaching, that it might be successful. This account, as we have received it from the ancients, we have thought fit to insert in our Ecclesiastical History.

THE VENERABLE BEDE

NOTES

8 *set to sale:* put up for sale. (O)
14 *fetching:* giving. (O)
17 *grace:* God's favour.
20 *becomes such to be:* is fitting that such people should be. (O)
23 *De Ira:* from anger. (Latin)
27 *repairing:* going. (O)
29 *ministers of the word:* people who would preach God's word.
35 *depart the city:* depart from the city; leave the city. (O)
38 *that:* so that; in order that. (O)

QUESTIONS

1 Who is 'the author of darkness' (line 15)? What did St Gregory contrast the English boys' 'fair countenances' with? And what did he contrast their 'graceful aspects' with?
2 St Gregory made a pun (play upon words that sound alike) when he was told that the boys came from the nation of the Angles. Explain this (line 20).
3 St Gregory also made puns on the name of the province from which the boys came, and the name of their king (lines 23 and 26). Explain these.
4 Why did St Gregory not go to England himself?

23 The Talented Man

This is a light piece by the humorous poet W. M. Praed (1802–39). It is supposed to be a letter from a lady in London to a lady in Lausanne, Switzerland. It describes how the lady writing the letter has met a 'talented' young poet who has just come up to London from Oxford University ('Brazennose College' is a college at Oxford, now usually called Brasenose College). The lady is so pleased to meet this young man whom everyone is talking about that she is not only prepared to overlook, but actually admires, all his faults—except one.

Dear Alice, you'll laugh when you know it—
   Last week, at the Duchess's ball,
I danced with the clever new poet,
   You've heard of him—Tully St Paul.
Miss Jonquil was perfectly frantic;
   I wish you had seen Lady Anne!
It really was very romantic;
   He *is* such a talented man!

He came up from Brazennose College,
   'Just caught', as they call it, last Spring;
And his head, love, is stuffed full of knowledge
   Of every conceivable thing:
Of science and logic he chatters,
   As fine and as fast as he can;
Though *I* am no judge of such matters,
   I'm sure he's a talented man.

His stories and jests are delightful—
   Not stories or jests, dear, for *you*—
The jests are exceedingly spiteful,
   The stories not always *quite* true.

Perhaps to be kind and veracious
    May do pretty well at Lausanne;
But it never would answer—good gracious!
    Chez nous, in a talented man.

He sneers—how my Alice would scold him!—
    At the bliss of a sigh or a tear:
He laughed—only think—when I told him
    How we cried o'er Trevelyan last year.
I vow I was quite in a passion;
    I broke all the sticks of my fan;
But sentiment's quite out of fashion,
    It seems, in a talented man.

Lady Bab, who is terribly moral,
    Declared that poor Tully is vain,
And apt—which is silly—to quarrel,
    And fond—which is wrong—of Champagne.
I listened and doubted, dear Alice;
    For I saw, when my Lady began,
It was only the Dowager's malice;
    She *does* hate a talented man!

He's hideous—I own it.—But fame, love,
    Is all that these eyes can adore:
He's lame—but Lord Byron was lame, love,
    And dumpy—but so is Tom Moore.
Then his voice—*such* a voice! my sweet creature,
    It's like your Aunt Lucy's Toucan;
But oh! what's a tone or a feature,
    When once one's a talented man?

My mother, you know, all the season,
    Has talked of Sir Geoffrey's estate;
And truly, to do the fool reason,
    He *has* been less horrid of late.

> But today, when we drive in the carriage,
>   I'll tell her to lay down her plan—
> If ever I venture on marriage,
>   It *must* be a talented man!
>
> P.S. I have found, on reflection,
>   One fault in my friend—*entre nous*—
> Without it he'd just be perfection—
>   Poor fellow—he has not a *sou*.
> And so, when he comes in September
>   To shoot with my Uncle, Sir Dan,
> I've promised Mamma to remember
>   He's only a talented man!

WINTHROP MACKWORTH PRAED

NOTES

 2 *ball:* dance.
14 *fine:* finely. (O)
23 *answer:* be successful; be suitable.
23 *good gracious!* an exclamation of surprise.
23 *chez nous:* where we live. (French)
28 *o'er:* over. (P)
28 *Trevelyan:* a popular sentimental novel of 1831.
41 *own:* admit.
44 *Tom Moore:* like Byron, an early nineteenth-century poet.
51 *to do the fool reason:* to be just to the fool. (O)
58 *entre nous:* between ourselves (as a secret). (French)
60 *has not a sou:* has no money at all. (A *sou* is an old French coin of small value.)

QUESTIONS

1 Why do you think Miss Jonquil was 'perfectly frantic' (line 5)? And why does the lady wish her friend had 'seen Lady Anne' (line 6)?
2 What kind of jests and stories does Tully St Paul tell? Do people in fashionable London admire him for these jests and stories?
3 Is Tully St Paul sentimental? Is the lady normally sentimental?
4 Why did the lady break the sticks of her fan?
5 What faults did Lady Bab find with Tully?

THE TALENTED MAN

6 What faults does the lady find with Tully in Verse 6? And how does she excuse these faults in him?
7 What does the lady decide in Verse 7?
8 Why does she change her mind in her postscript (Verse 8)? And why does she say in the last line that Tully is '*only* a talented man'?

24 A Love-Poet

Dr Samuel Johnson (1709–84) was the outstanding writer of the middle years of the eighteenth century. He wrote books of many different kinds, all of them distinguished by their strong good sense, including a story called *Rasselas*, of which we have an extract later in this volume (Passage 29), and a book called *Lives of the Poets* (1779–81), from which the following piece is taken. In *Lives of the Poets*, Johnson describes the lives and work of fifty-two English poets of the previous 150 years or so. This piece comes from his 'Life of Edmund Waller', a poet who lived from 1606 to 1687. It is a typical and delightful extract, full of Johnson's good humour and accurate knowledge of people.

[The next piece in this volume is a passage from a modern biography (book about the life) of Dr Johnson.]

Waller was not one of those idolaters of praise who cultivate their minds at the expense of their fortunes. Rich as he was by inheritance, he took care early to grow richer by marrying Mrs Banks, a great heiress in the city, whom the interest of the court was employed to obtain for Mr Crofts. Having brought him a son, who died young, and a daughter, who was afterwards married to Mr Dormer of Oxfordshire, she died in childbed, and left him a widower of about five-and-twenty, gay and wealthy, to please himself with another marriage.

Being too young to resist beauty, and probably too vain to think himself resistible, he fixed his heart, perhaps half fondly and half ambitiously, upon the Lady Dorothea Sidney, eldest daughter of the Earl of Leicester, whom he courted by all the poetry in which Sacharissa is celebrated; the name is derived from the Latin appellation of *sugar*, and implies, if it means anything, a spiritless mildness, and dull good-nature, such as excites rather tenderness than esteem, and such as, though always treated with kindness, is never honoured or admired.

Yet he describes Sacharissa as a sublime, predominating beauty, of lofty charms, and imperious influence, on whom he looks with amazement rather than fondness, whose chains he wishes, though in vain, to break, and whose presence is 'wine' that 'inflames to madness'.

His acquaintance with this high-born dame gave wit no opportunity of boasting its influence; she was not to be subdued by the powers of verse, but rejected his addresses, it is said, with disdain, and drove him away to solace his disappointment with Amoret or Phillis. She married in 1639 the Earl of Sunderland, who died at Newbury in the King's cause; and, in her old age, meeting somewhere with Waller, asked him when he would again write such verses upon her: 'When you are as young, Madam,' said he, 'and as handsome as you were then.'

When he had lost all hopes of Sacharissa, he looked round him for an easier conquest, and gained a lady of the family of Bresse, or Breaux. The time of his marriage is not exactly known. It has not been discovered that his wife was won by his poetry; nor is anything told of her, but that she brought him many children. He doubtless praised some whom he would have been afraid to marry; and perhaps married one whom he would have been ashamed to praise. Many qualities contribute to domestic happiness, upon which poetry has no colours to bestow, and many airs and sallies may delight imagination, which he who flatters them never can approve. There are charms made only for distant admiration. No spectacle is nobler than a blaze.

SAMUEL JOHNSON

NOTES

4 *interest:* influence.
4 *court:* royal court.
11 *resistible:* capable of being resisted.
16 *excites:* arouses.
25 *addresses:* wooing; proposals of marriage.
39 *upon which poetry has no colours to bestow:* which poetry cannot improve.
40 *airs:* graceful (or sometimes foolish) ways of behaving.

QUESTIONS

1 Explain the following phrases:

  a 'those idolaters of praise who cultivate their minds at the expense of their fortunes' (lines 1–2).
  b 'too vain to think himself resistible' (lines 10–11).

  c 'a spiritless mildness and dull good-nature' (lines 15–16).
  d 'a sublime, predominating beauty' (line 19).
  e 'gave wit no opportunity of boasting its influence' (lines 23–4).
2 Why does Johnson think 'Sacharissa' was the wrong name for Waller to give the lady he described in the love-poems dedicated to her?
3 Explain Waller's answer to Lady Dorothea Sidney, when he met her as an old woman (lines 29–31).
4 Does Johnson think that the qualities in a woman that it is natural to praise in poetry are the qualities that make a man want to marry a woman? Give reasons for your answer.
5 The last sentence of this passage ('No spectacle is nobler than a blaze') is a very well-known remark of Johnson's. How does it illustrate what he has said in the previous sentence ('There are charms made only for distant admiration')?

25 A Portrait of Dr Johnson

Dr Johnson was not only a remarkable writer, but made a very strong personal impression on everyone who met him. His friend James Boswell wrote a book about him in which he recorded all he could of the marvellous conversations they had had together during the years they knew each other: *The Life of Samuel Johnson*. (There is an extract in Book 2.) Here is a passage from a book about Johnson called *Dr Johnson and Company* by a modern writer and journalist, Robert Lynd. Lynd draws together in his book descriptions of Johnson by many people who knew him. Among those mentioned here are William Hogarth, a well-known painter; Samuel Richardson, the author of one of the first English novels, *Pamela*; and Sir Joshua Reynolds, a famous portrait-painter and the first president of the Royal Academy of Arts. Anthony Trollope and Robert Louis Stevenson, who are also mentioned in this extract, were nineteenth-century novelists who both published many books.

Dr Johnson survives in literary history as the king—nay, the emperor—of good company: yet few men of genius have seemed less fitted in some respects for the pleasures of society. He had the use of only one eye. His figure, according to Boswell, was 'unwieldy from corpulency' and, whether he was in company or walking along the street, he added to the grotesque effect by startling, convulsive gestures, like those of a man suffering from St Vitus's dance. Even when he was a young man, his appearance had been found 'very forbidding' by the woman who was to become his wife. Hogarth's account of his first glimpse of Johnson as a young man was even more uncomplimentary. One day, when he called to see Samuel Richardson, 'he perceived a person standing at a window in the room, shaking his head and rolling himself about in a strange ridiculous manner. He concluded that he was an idiot, whom his relations had put under the care of Mr Richardson as a very good man.' The supposed idiot was Johnson. A minor poet of the age wrote of him as unflatteringly:

> To view him, porters with their loads would rest
> And babes cling frighted to the nurse's breast.

And his habits were at times as eccentric and grotesque as his appearance. Boswell, in order to bring him to life, has spared us none of these oddities of behaviour, and he does not shrink from something like caricature in his account of Johnson's facial and bodily contortions during conversation. 'In the intervals of articulating,' he says, 'he made various sounds with his mouth, sometimes as if ruminating, or what is called chewing the cud, sometimes giving a half whistle, sometimes making his tongue play backward from the roof of his mouth, as if clucking like a hen, and sometimes protruding it against his upper gums in front as if pronouncing quickly under his breath, *too, too, too*; all this accompanied sometimes with a thoughtful look, but more frequently with a smile. Generally, when he had concluded a period, in the course of a dispute, by which he was a good deal exhausted by violence and vociferation, he used to blow out his breath like a whale.'

And if Johnson's uncouthness, untidiness and eccentric habits seemed to unfit him to play the part of a social idol, he had other qualities that were no more likely to make him welcome either in the tavern or in the drawing-room. He was not only of a naturally gloomy disposition, but was often irritable, surly and indifferent to the feelings of his friends and acquaintances. His gloom may have been the result of his lifelong disease, or may have been inherited, as he thought, from his father. 'I inherited,' he told Boswell, 'a vile melancholy from my father, which has made me mad all my life, at least not sober.'

It is only when we realize how unfitted in many respects Johnson was for society that we can understand how prodigious is the position that he occupies in the affections of men and women today. Poor, repulsively ugly, uncouth, with disgusting table-manners, surly, irascible, a bully, intolerant, dirty, slovenly and ridiculous in dress, eccentric, unhealthy, morbid and gloomy, haunted by a bad conscience, tormented by the fear of insanity and death—one would say it was the portrait of a sour misanthropist, doomed to avoid and to be avoided by his fellow men. Johnson, on the other hand, had scarcely a defect that was not more than counterbalanced by a corresponding virtue. Even those who, on first meeting him, found him awkward and repellent were usually convinced before they parted from him that he was the most enchanting companion alive. His churlishness was exceeded by his charity. He was dictatorial, but, equally, he loved to give pleasure. Though he may have flouted the graces, no man set a higher value on them. He was as courteous as he was ill-mannered. He was no more gloomy than he was playful. His very morbidity of mind, instead of making him shrink from company, drove him into company as the only refuge from his haunting fears.

I doubt if any other man of genius ever lived to whom company was so necessary as it was to Dr Johnson. 'Solitude to him,' says Sir Joshua Reynolds, 'was horror; nor would he ever trust himself alone but when employed in writing or reading. He has often begged me to go home with him to prevent his being alone in the coach. Any company was better than none.'

Hence the extraordinary variety of the company in his biography. He could associate without envy with other men of genius, and at the same time was equally at home (in Reynolds's phrase) with 'many mean persons whose presence he could command'. It might be said of him that it was only in company and in conversation that he was a man with ten talents making full use of them all.

He was a man who found his true vocation, not in his work, but in his leisure. He was most active when he was most slothful, and never wasted his time less than when he was wasting his time. Conversation has often been recognized as an art, but never as a profession, and, because it is not one of the activities by which men customarily earn a livelihood, Johnson constantly reproached himself with indolence. When we reflect on the matter, however, there seems to be some flaw in the code of morality which would commend the literary industry of Trollope and would condemn the conversational industry of Johnson. The world has not gained less from this than from that, and, if we judge by results, it is difficult to agree with Johnson's denunciation of himself as an idler.

He was certainly no idler as a student of the art of conversation. He practised talking as assiduously as Stevenson practised writing. He told Reynolds that he had 'a rule, which he said he always practised on every occasion, of speaking his best, whether the person to whom he addressed himself was or was not capable of comprehending him'. His genius as a conversationalist was not the fruit of indolence, but was, as much as any other kind of genius, due to an infinite capacity for taking pains. He had a mind which, as Reynolds said, was 'always ready for use', and the most variously stored mind of his age. While not conventionally studious, he was a supremely great student of life, manners and literature. And all that he had learned, though he could not put it on paper, he could produce at a moment's notice in a tavern or over a cup of tea.

ROBERT LYND

NOTES

7 *St Vitus's dance:* disease of the nerves, which causes the body to make sudden, uncontrolled movements.
18 *frighted:* frightened. (O)
31 *period:* full, usually complex sentence.
71 *mean:* low-class.
92 *taking pains:* taking trouble; trying hard.

QUESTIONS

1 If you are in class, let various members of the class imitate the sounds made by Dr Johnson, according to Boswell's description in lines 23-33.
2 Robert Lynd's portrait of Dr Johnson is made up largely of contrasts. In lines 52-9 he says that Johnson seemed 'awkward and repellent' on first meeting, showed 'churlishness', was 'dictatorial', 'flouted the graces', and was 'ill-mannered' and 'gloomy'. List the qualities he had in contrast to all these characteristics, according to Lynd.
3 Why did Johnson depend so much on the company of other people, in Lynd's opinion?
4 What does Lynd mean by saying (lines 75-6) 'He was most active when he was most slothful, and never wasted his time less than when he was wasting his time'?
5 Do you think that Johnson's rule, 'of speaking his best, whether the person to whom he addressed himself was or was not capable of comprehending him', was a good rule?

26 The Song of the Shirt

Although Britain as a whole became a rich country in the nineteenth century because of her industrial progress, it was also a period in which many poor people suffered badly, especially in the towns. Some writers tried to draw attention to this fact, and to awaken their readers' consciences about it. The following poem had a great effect when published in the magazine *Punch* in 1843. Its author was Thomas Hood (1799-1845), who was also a journalist and humorous writer.

> With fingers weary and worn,
>   With eyelids heavy and red,
> A woman sat, in unwomanly rags,
>   Plying her needle and thread—
>   Stitch—stitch—stitch!
>   In poverty, hunger, and dirt,
> And still with a voice of dolorous pitch
>   She sang the 'Song of the Shirt'!
>
>   'Work—work—work!
> While the cock is crowing aloof;
>   And work—work—work
> Till the stars shine through the roof!
> It's oh! to be a slave
>   Along with the barbarous Turk,
> Where woman has never a soul to save,
>   If this were Christian work!
>
>   'Work—work—work
> Till the brain begins to swim;
>   Work—work—work
> Till the eyes are heavy and dim!

Seam, and gusset, and band—
    Band, and gusset, and seam,
Till over the buttons I fall asleep,
    And sew them on in a dream!

'Oh! men with sisters dear!
    Oh! men with mothers and wives!
It is not linen you're wearing out,
    But human creatures' lives!
    Stitch—stitch—stitch,
    In poverty, hunger, and dirt,
Sewing at once with a double thread
    A shroud as well as a shirt.

'But why do I talk of death!
    That phantom of grisly bone,
I hardly fear his terrible shape,
    It seems so like my own—
    It seems so like my own,
    Because of the fasts I keep;
O God! that bread should be so dear,
    And flesh and blood so cheap!

'Work—work—work!
My labour never flags;
    And what are its wages? A bed of straw,
A crust of bread—and rags.
That shattered roof—and this naked floor—
    A table—a broken chair—
And a wall so blank, my shadow I thank
    For sometimes falling there.

'Work—work—work!
From weary chime to chime,
    Work—work—work
As prisoners work for crime!

Band, and gusset, and seam,
   Seam, and gusset, and band,
Till the heart is sick, and the brain benumbed,
   As well as the weary hand.

   'Work—work—work,
In the dull December light,
   And work—work—work,
When the weather is warm and bright— 60
While underneath the eaves
   The brooding swallows cling,
As if to show me their sunny backs
   And twit me with the spring.

'Oh! but to breathe the breath
   Of the cowslip and primrose sweet—
With the sky above my head,
   And the grass beneath my feet!
For only one short hour
   To feel as I used to feel, 70
Before I knew the woes of want
   And the walk that costs a meal!

'Oh! but for one short hour!
   A respite however brief!
No blessed leisure for love or hope,
   But only time for grief!
A little weeping would ease my heart,
   But in their briny bed
My tears must stop, for every drop
   Hinders needle and thread!' 80

With fingers weary and worn,
   With eyelids heavy and red,
A woman sat, in unwomanly rags,
   Plying her needle and thread—
      Stitch—stitch—stitch!

> In poverty, hunger, and dirt,
> And still with a voice of dolorous pitch—
> Would that its tone could reach the rich!—
> She sang this 'Song of the Shirt'!
>
> THOMAS HOOD

NOTES

18 *swim:* seem to be moving round and round.
47 *my shadow I thank:* I thank my shadow. (P)
71 *want:* lack; not having enough to live on. (O)
88 *would that:* I wish that. (O or P)

QUESTIONS

1. What does Hood mean by the phrase 'unwomanly rags' in line 3?
2. What time of day is referred to in the line 'While the cock is crowing aloof' (line 10)? Put into your own words the meaning of lines 9–12.
3. What is meant by the lines

    > It is not linen you're wearing out,
    > But human creatures' lives

    (lines 27–8)?
4. Why does the woman say (lines 31–2) that she is sewing 'a shroud as well as a shirt'?
5. Why does the 'shape' of death seem to the woman like her own shape?
6. Why is the woman grateful to her shadow?
7. What does the woman mean (line 72) by 'the walk that costs a meal'?
8. Why can the woman not even weep?
9. What is the effect of the repetitions, like 'Stitch—stitch—stitch', in this poem? List the other repetitions which have this effect.
10. There is one more line in the last verse than in all the others. Which is the extra, unexpected line? Is it an important one?

27 Parson Adams Has a Fight

This is an extract from one of the first great comic novels in English, *Joseph Andrews* by Henry Fielding (1707–54). It was published in 1742. Its chief characters are two good but rather simple men, the young servant Joseph Andrews and his friend Parson Adams. In their travels round England these two meet all kinds of rough and selfish people, and are always getting into trouble by trying to do what they think is right. But they always remain innocent and lovable, and their adventures are usually more amusing than tragic. At the beginning of this extract Joseph and Parson Adams have just arrived at an inn where they are stopping for dinner. Joseph is travelling on Adams's horse, while Adams is travelling by coach, along with Mrs Slipslop and several other passengers.

As soon as the passengers had alighted from the coach, Mr Adams, as was his custom, made directly to the kitchen, where he found Joseph sitting by the fire, and the hostess anointing his leg: for the horse which Mr Adams had borrowed of his clerk had so violent a propensity to kneeling that one would have thought that it had been his trade as well as his master's. Nor would he always give any notice of such his intention; he was often found on his knees when the rider least expected it. This foible however was of no great inconvenience to the parson, who was accustomed to it, and as his legs almost touched the ground when he bestrode the beast, had but a little way to fall, and threw himself forward on such occasions with so much dexterity that he never received any mischief; the horse and he frequently rolling many paces' distance, and afterwards both getting up and meeting as good friends as ever.

Poor Joseph, who had not been used to such kind of cattle, though an excellent horseman, did not so happily disengage himself: but falling with his leg under the beast received a violent contusion, to which the good woman was, as we have said, applying a warm hand with some camphorated spirits just at the time when the parson entered the kitchen.

He had scarce expressed his concern for Joseph's misfortune, before the host likewise entered. This surly fellow, who always proportioned his respect to the appearance of a traveller, from 'God bless your honour' down to plain 'Coming presently', observing his wife on her knees to a footman, cried out, without considering his circumstances, 'What a pox is the woman about? Why don't you mind the company in the coach? Go and ask them what they will have for dinner.' 'My dear,' says she, 'you know they can have nothing but what is at the fire, which will be ready presently; and really the poor young man's leg is very much bruised.' At which words, she fell to chafing more violently than before; the bell then happening to ring, he damned his wife and bid her go in to the company, and not stand rubbing there all day: for he did not believe the young fellow's leg was so bad as he pretended, and if it was, within twenty miles he would find a surgeon to cut it off. Upon these words Adams fetched two strides across the room; and snapping his fingers over his head, muttered aloud, He would excommunicate such a wretch for a farthing, for he believed the Devil had more humanity. These words occasioned a dialogue between Adams and the host, in which there were two or three sharp replies, till Joseph bade the latter know how to behave himself to his betters. At which the host (having first strictly surveyed Adams) scornfully repeated the word 'betters', flew into a rage, and telling Joseph he was as able to walk out of his house as he had been to walk into it, offered to lay violent hands on him; which perceiving, Adams dealt him so sound a compliment over his face with his fist that the blood immediately gushed out of his nose in a stream. The host being unwilling to be outdone in courtesy, especially by a person of Adams's figure, returned the favour with so much gratitude that the parson's nostrils likewise began to look a little redder than usual. Upon which he again assailed his antagonist, and with another stroke laid him sprawling on the floor.

The hostess, who was a better wife than so surly a husband deserved, seeing her husband all bloody and stretched along, hastened presently to his assistance, or rather to revenge the blow, which, to all appearance, was the last he would ever receive; when, lo! a pan full of hog's blood, which unluckily stood on the dresser, presented itself first to her hands. She seized it in her fury, and without any reflection discharged it into the parson's face, and with so good an aim that much the greater part first saluted his countenance, and trickled thence in so large a current down his beard, and over his garments, that a more horrible spectacle was hardly to be seen, or even imagined. All which was perceived by Mrs Slipslop, who entered the kitchen at that instant. This good gentlewoman, not being of a temper so extremely cool and patient as perhaps was required to ask many questions on this occasion, flew with great impetuosity at the hostess's cap, which, together with some of her hair, she plucked from her head in a moment, giving her at the same time several hearty cuffs in the face, which, by frequent practice on the inferior servants, she had learned an excellent knack of delivering with a good grace. Poor Joseph could hardly rise from his chair; the parson was employed in wiping the blood from his eyes, which had entirely blinded him, and the landlord was but just beginning to stir, whilst Mrs Slipslop, holding down the landlady's face with her left hand, made so dexterous a use of her right, that the poor woman began to roar in a key, which alarmed all the company in the inn.

There happened to be in the inn at this time, besides the ladies who arrived in the stage coach, three gentlemen, all whom the horrid outcry of murder presently brought into the kitchen, where the several combatants were found in the postures already described.

It was now no difficulty to put an end to the fray, the conquerors being satisfied with the vengeance they had taken, and the conquered having no appetite to renew the fight. The principal figure, and which engaged the eyes of all, was Adams, who was all over covered with blood, which the company concluded to be his own; and consequently imagined him no longer for this world. But the host, who had now recovered from his blow, and was risen from the ground, soon delivered them from this apprehension, by damning his wife for wasting the hog's puddings, and telling her all would have been very well, if she had not intermeddled like a b . . . as she was; adding he was very glad the gentlewoman had paid her, though not half what she deserved.

HENRY FIELDING

NOTES

2 *made . . . to:* went to; started to go to.
4 *of:* from. (O)
7 *such his intention:* such an intention on his part; his intention to do this. (O)
12 *mischief:* damage; harm.
15 *such kind:* such a kind; such kinds. (O)
15 *cattle:* animals. (O)
16 *happily:* fortunately.
21 *scarce:* scarcely; hardly. (O)
23 *your honour:* a respectful way of addressing a gentleman.

24 *presently:* at once. (O)
26 *what a pox:* an offensive, emphatic way of saying 'whatever'. 'Pox' is a disease. (O and V)
26 *mind:* look after; see to.
30 *fell to:* began.
35 *fetched:* took. (O)
44 *which perceiving:* perceiving which. (O)
45 *sound:* thorough.
53 *along:* out. (O)
72 *stir:* move.
74 *key:* musical key; range of musical notes.
77 *stage coach:* public coach for passengers and mail, corresponding to buses and trains between towns nowadays.
78 *the several:* each of the.
89 *b . . . :* bitch (female dog), which is a rude word for a woman. (V)

QUESTIONS

1 Explain the following phrases:
  a 'had so violent a propensity to kneeling that one would have thought that it had been his trade as well as his master's' (lines 4-6).
  b 'his legs almost touched the ground when he bestrode the beast' (lines 9-10).
  c 'always proportioned his respect to the appearance of a traveller' (lines 22-3).
  d 'Joseph bade the latter know how to behave himself to his betters' (lines 40-1).
  e 'saluted his countenance' (line 59).
  f 'by frequent practice on the inferior servants' (lines 67-8).
  g 'soon delivered them from this apprehension' (lines 86-7).
2 How had Joseph hurt his leg?
3 Why was the host of the inn angry when he saw his wife attending to Joseph's leg?
4 Why did Parson Adams first speak sharply to the host?
5 Why did Parson Adams first hit the host?
6 What does the author mean when he says (line 47) that the host was 'unwilling to be outdone in courtesy'? Is this the usual meaning of 'courtesy'? Why does the author express himself here in this way?
7 How do we know that the hostess 'was a better wife than so surly a husband deserved' (line 52)?
8 What did the company think when they saw Parson Adams covered with blood?
9 What did the host think about Mrs Slipslop's attack on his wife?

28 London at War—and After

Sir Harold Nicolson (1886–1968) was a diplomat and politician who was also an interesting writer. He was very friendly with many of the members of upper-class society, but he also held strong democratic views, and for some years was a Member of Parliament supporting the Labour (or Socialist) Party. He kept a diary (a daily record of events) for long periods of his life, and this was published shortly before he died. It describes both his own moods and impressions, and also much news and gossip that he heard in the political and social world in which he lived. So it gives a lively idea, very often, of the atmosphere of the years it covers.

Here we have three extracts from the volume published under the title *Diaries and Letters 1939–45*. The first describes a day in the early part of the Second World War. 'They' in the second sentence refers, of course, to the Germans, 'we' to the British. The 'siren' was the signal that a bombing raid by enemy aeroplanes was beginning. The first part of the day was spent by Nicolson at his home in the country outside London, and in the afternoon he went up to London, where he also had rooms in a building (mainly occupied by lawyers) called the Temple. At this time, besides being a Member of Parliament, Nicolson was also giving a talk on the radio every week, which he refers to in this passage. The second extract describes a day in 1941, almost a year later. The war was of course still on, and Nicolson had spent the previous night 'fire-watching'—that is to say, staying up and walking around to report any fires that might have been started by a bombing raid. The balloons he mentions were 'barrage balloons'—big balloons that flew high in the sky on wire cords to prevent German aeroplanes flying low over the city. On this day, Nicolson went to a political meeting in the Midlands, where women told him about their difficulties. (Lord Woolton was a Government Minister in charge of food supplies.) The third extract describes London a month or so after the war against Germany ended in 1945. A general election was being held (which the Labour Party won). 'Winston' here means Winston Churchill, who was the leader of the Conservative Party, and Prime Minister during the war.

26 August 1940

A lovely morning. They raided London yesterday, and we raided Berlin. I work at my broadcast talk. At noon I hear aeroplanes and shortly afterwards the wail of the siren. People are becoming quite used to these interruptions. I find one practises a sort of suspension of the imagination. I do not think that that drone in the sky means death to many people at any moment. It seems so incredible as I sit here at my window, looking out on the fuchsias and the zinneas with yellow butterflies circling in the air intent on murdering each other. One lives in the present. The past is too sad a recollection and the future too sad a despair.

I go up to London. After dinner I walk back to the Temple. It is a strange experience. London is as dark as the stage at Vicenza after all the lights have been put out. Vague gleamings of architecture. It is warm and the stars straddle the sky like grains of rice. Then the searchlights come on, each terminating in a swab of cotton-wool which is its own mist-area. Suburban guns thump and boom. In the centre there are no guns, only a drone of aeroplanes, which may be enemy or not. A few lonely footsteps hurry along the Strand. A little nervous man catches up with me and starts a conversation. I embarrass him by asking him to have a cigarette and pausing lengthily while I light it. His hand trembles. Mine does not.

When I get into my rooms, I turn the lights off and sit at the window. There is still a drone of 'planes, and from time to time a dull thump in the distance. I turn on my lights and write this, but I hear more 'planes coming and must darken everything and listen in the night. I have no sense of fear whatsoever. Is this fatalism or what? It is very beautiful. I wait and listen. There are more drones and then the searchlights switch out and the all-clear goes. I shut my shutters, turn on my lights and finish this. The clocks of London strike midnight. I go to bed.

25 July 1941

After fire-watching all night in the House of Commons, I get up at 5 a.m. and walk down to the Temple. It is a beautiful morning. The river is swollen high and heaves slightly under a pink satin sky. The balloons are going up slowly all over London—at first clumsy tadpoles, and then, as they reach the upper air, little minnows flashing silver in the sun.

I dictate letters and then go up to Leicester. Rain lashes against the hot windows and the cornfields lean over into inconvenient shapes. I have a women's meeting first. They concentrate upon the troubles of the housewife. Eggs are torn from the hens and sent to places from which they are packed into crates labelled 'new laid' and then placed in railway-trucks labelled 'immediate' and kept in sidings for three hot weeks. Lord Woolton is not liked. Was it not he (the Napoleon of the multiple store) who said that they should all make plum jam? Where are the plums? Lord Woolton does not know.

24 July 1945

William Jowitt is at the Beefsteak. He says he has no idea at all how the Election has gone. Some people feel that there has been a wide swing to the left and that a Labour Government will be returned. Others imagine that Winston will be back with a fifty-seats majority.

I leave about 10.30 and am astonished to find a completely different London. For years I have crept out of the Club with my torch, seeking and peering for the little step on the threshold. Tonight I emerged into a London coruscating with lights like Stockholm. My old way along the Embankment from the Temple Station, which I have traversed such countless times, feeling my way between the surface shelters and the trees, was lit up by a thousand arc-lights. All these were turned up on 15 July when double-summer-time ended. I had not realized what a transfiguration had been achieved. Meanwhile all the sticky stuff has been removed from the windows of the buses and undergrounds and we shall no longer remember how we used to peep out through a little diamond slit in the texture to read the names of the stations as they flashed by. One forgets these things at once.

HAROLD NICOLSON

NOTES

17 *mist-area:* area of mist in the sky lit up by the searchlight.
19 *the Strand:* a street in London near the Temple.
29 *all-clear:* the signal given by the sirens to show that the danger had passed.
43 *'new laid':* recently laid by the hens.
49 *the Beefsteak:* the name of a London club.
51 *returned:* voted into power by the electors.
57 *the Embankment:* the north bank of the Thames between the Houses of Parliament and the City of London.
58 *surface shelters:* air-raid shelters above the ground.
60 *double-summer-time:* clocks used to be put forward an hour in spring in order to lengthen the amount of daylight in the evenings. This was known as British Summer Time. During the war, clocks were put forward another hour in summer in order to get even more daylight in the evenings. This was called 'double-summer-time'.

64 *diamond slit:* bus and train windows were covered over during the war, so that light would not shine out and be seen by enemy planes. Narrow diamond-shaped holes (slits) were left, through which people could look out and see where the bus was.

QUESTIONS

1 The first sentence in the first extract says 'A lovely morning' (meaning the weather); the second records bombing raids by the British and the Germans. This and the second extract are full of such contrasts between the beautiful and peaceful appearance of the world, and the cruelties of war. Find all the other examples of such contrasts. (What do the 'yellow butterflies' in line 9 refer to?)
2 What does Nicolson mean by 'Vague gleamings of architecture' (line 14)?
3 Where were the anti-aircraft guns that defended London?
4 Why was the man in the Strand (lines 19–22) embarrassed by Nicolson's offer of a cigarette?
5 Tadpoles (baby frogs, before they have acquired legs) are black; minnows are small silver fish. Why does Nicolson say (lines 36–8) that the barrage balloons looked first like the one, then like the other?
6 Why did the women at the meeting in Leicester not like Lord Woolton?
7 In what way did Nicolson find London 'completely different' when he came out of his club on 24 July 1945?
8 Do you agree with Nicolson that we are quick to forget difficulties and discomforts when they have passed?

29 The History of a Man of Learning

Dr Johnson (see Passages Nos. 24 and 25 in this book) wrote *Rasselas* in 1759. He wrote it in one week, in order to pay for the expenses of his mother's funeral and to pay her debts. It tells the story of an Abyssinian prince called Rasselas who goes to Egypt with his sister, Princess Nekayah, and the aged philosopher Imlac. In Egypt the three of them study the different ways men choose to live. They find that very few men are happy. In this passage Imlac tells the story of a learned astronomer whom he met. This man seemed at first to be one of the few happy men on earth—but Imlac slowly realized, as we shall see, that he had gone mad.

They returned to Cairo, and were so well pleased at finding themselves together, that none of them went much abroad. The prince began to love learning, and one day declared to Imlac, that he intended to devote himself to science, and pass the rest of his days in literary solitude.

'Before you make your final choice,' answered Imlac, 'you ought to examine its hazards, and converse with some of those who are grown old in the company of themselves. I have just left the observatory of one of the most learned astronomers in the world, who has spent forty years in unwearied attention to the motions and appearances of the celestial bodies, and has drawn out his soul in endless calculations. He admits a few friends once a month to hear his deductions and enjoy his discoveries. I was introduced as a man of knowledge worthy of his notice. Men of various ideas and fluent conversation are commonly welcome to those whose thoughts have been long fixed upon a single point, and who find the images of other things stealing away. I delighted him with my remarks; he smiled at the narrative of my travels, and was glad to forget the constellations and descend for a moment into the lower world.

'On the next day of vacation I renewed my visit, and was so fortunate as to please him again. He relaxed from that time the severity of his rule, and permitted me to enter at my own choice. I found him always busy, and always glad to be relieved. As each knew much which the other was desirous of learning, we exchanged our notions with great delight. I perceived that I had every day more of his confidence, and always found new cause of admiration in the profundity of his mind. His comprehension is vast, his memory capacious and retentive, his discourse is methodical, and his expression clear.

'His integrity and benevolence are equal to his learning. His deepest researches and most favourite studies are willingly interrupted for any opportunity of doing good by his counsel or his riches. To his closest retreat, at his most busy moments, all are admitted that want his assistance: "For though I exclude idleness and pleasure, I will never," says he, "bar my doors against charity. To man is permitted the contemplation of the skies, but the practice of virtue is commanded."'

'Surely,' said the princess, 'this man is happy.'

'I visited him,' said Imlac, 'with more and more frequency, and was every time more enamoured of his conversation; he was sublime without haughtiness, courteous without formality, and communicative without ostentation. I was at first, great princess, of your opinion, thought him the happiest of mankind, and often congratulated him on the blessing that he enjoyed. He seemed to hear nothing with indifference but the praises of his condition, to which he always returned a general answer, and diverted the conversation to some other topic.

'Amidst this willingness to be pleased and labour to please, I had quickly reason to imagine that some painful sentiment pressed upon his mind. He often looked up earnestly towards the sun, and let his voice fall in the midst of his discourse. He would sometimes, when we were alone, gaze upon me in silence, with the air of a man who longed to speak what he was yet resolved to suppress. He would often send for me with vehement injunctions of haste, though, when I came to him, he had nothing extraordinary to say; and sometimes, when I was leaving him, would call me back, pause a few moments, and then dismiss me.

'At last the time came when the secret burst his reserve. We were sitting together last night in the turret of his house, watching the emersion of a satellite of Jupiter. A sudden tempest clouded the sky, and disappointed our observation. We sat awhile silent in the dark, and then he addressed himself to me in these words: "Imlac, I have long considered thy friendship as the greatest blessing of my life. Integrity without knowledge is weak and useless, and knowledge without integrity is dangerous and dreadful. I have found in thee all the qualities requisite for trust—benevolence, experience, and fortitude.

I have long discharged an office which I must soon quit at the call of nature, and shall rejoice in the hour of imbecility and pain to devolve it upon thee."

'I thought myself honoured by this testimony, and protested that whatever could conduce to his happiness would add likewise to mine.

' "Hear, Imlac, what thou wilt not without difficulty credit. I have possessed for five years the regulation of the weather, and the distribution of the seasons; the sun has listened to my dictates, and passed from tropic to tropic by my direction; the clouds, at my call, have poured their waters, and the Nile has overflowed at my command; I have restrained the rage of the dog-star, and mitigated the fervours of the crab. The winds alone, of all the elemental powers, have hitherto refused my authority and multitudes have perished by equinoctial tempests which I found myself unable to prohibit or restrain. I have administered this great office with exact justice, and made to the different nations of the earth an impartial dividend of rain and sunshine. What must have been the misery of half the globe, is I had limited the clouds to particular regions, or confined the sun to either side of the equator?"

'I suppose he discovered in me, through the obscurity of the room, some tokens of amazement and doubt, for, after a short pause, he proceeded thus:

' "Not to be easily credited will neither surprise nor offend me; for I am, probably, the first of human beings to whom this trust has been imparted. Nor do I know whether to deem this distinction a reward or punishment; since I have possessed it, I have been far less happy than before, and nothing but the consciousness of good intention could have enabled me to support the weariness of unremitted vigilance."

' "How long, sir," said I, "has this great office been in your hands?"

' "About ten years ago," said he, "my daily observations of the changes of the sky led me to consider, whether, if I had the power of the seasons, I could confer greater plenty upon the inhabitants of the earth. This contemplation fastened on my mind, and I sat days and nights in imaginary dominion, pouring upon this country and that the showers of fertility and seconding every fall of rain with a due proportion of sunshine. I had yet only the will to do good, and did not imagine that I should ever have the power.

' "One day, as I was looking on the fields withering with heat, I felt in my mind a sudden wish that I could send rain on the southern mountains, and raise the Nile to an inundation. In the hurry of my imagination I commanded rain to fall; and by comparing the time of my command with that of the inundation, I found that the clouds had listened to my lips."

' "Might not some other cause," said I, "produce this concurrence? the Nile does not always rise on the same day."

' "Do not believe," said he with impatience, "that such objections could escape me; I reasoned long against my own conviction, and laboured against truth with the utmost obstinacy. I sometimes suspected myself of madness, and should not have dared to impart this secret but to a man like you, capable of distinguishing the wonderful from the impossible, and the incredible from the false."

' "Why, sir," said I, "do you call that incredible, which you know, or think you know, to be true?"

' "Because," said he, "I cannot prove it by any external evidence; and I know too well the laws of demonstration to think that my conviction ought to influence another, who cannot like me be conscious of its force. I therefore shall not attempt to gain credit by disputation. It is sufficient that I feel this power, that I have long possessed, and every day exerted it. But the life of man is short, the infirmities of age increase upon me, and the time will soon come when the regulator of the year must mingle with the dust. The care of appointing a successor has long disturbed me; the night and the day have been spent in comparisons of all the characters which have come to my knowledge, and I have yet found none so worthy as thyself."

' "Hear, therefore, what I shall impart, with attention such as the welfare of a world requires. If the task of a king be considered as difficult, who has the care only of a few millions, to whom he cannot do much good or harm, what must be the anxiety of him on whom depends the action of the elements, and the great gifts of light and heat! Hear me therefore with attention.

' "I have diligently considered the position of the earth and sun, and formed innumerable schemes in which I changed their situation. I have sometimes turned aside the axis of the earth, and sometimes varied the ecliptic of the sun; but I have found it impossible to make a disposition by which the world may be advantaged; what one region gains, another loses by any imaginable alteration, even without considering the distant parts of the solar system with which we are unacquainted. Do not, therefore, in thy administration of the year, indulge thy pride by innovation; do not please thyself with thinking that thou canst make thyself renowned to all future ages by disordering the seasons. The memory of mischief is no desirable fame. Much less will it become thee to let kindness or interest prevail. Never rob other countries of rain to pour it on thine own. For us the Nile is sufficient."

'I promised, that when I possessed the power, I would use it with inflexible integrity; and he dismissed me, pressing my hand. "My heart," said he, "will be now at rest, and my benevolence will no more destroy my quiet; I have found a man of wisdom and virtue, to whom I can cheerfully bequeath the inheritance of the sun."'

The prince heard this narration with very serious regard; but the princess smiled, and Pekuah convulsed herself with laughter. 'Ladies,' said Imlac, 'to mock the heaviest of human affliction is neither charitable nor wise. Few can attain this man's knowledge, and few practise his virtues; but all may suffer his calamity. Of the uncertainties of our present state, the most dreadful and alarming is the uncertain continuance of reason.'

The princess was recollected, and the favourite was abashed. Rasselas, more deeply affected, inquired of Imlac, whether he thought such maladies of the mind frequent, and how they were contracted.

SAMUEL JOHNSON

NOTES

- 7 *are grown:* have grown. (O)
- 11 *drawn out his soul:* spent much mental energy.
- 17 *stealing:* going slowly and quietly.
- 31 *closest:* most private. (O)
- 32 *retreat:* place where one can go when one does not want to be disturbed.
- 58 *emersion:* emerging; emergence; coming into view. (O)
- 65 *discharged:* carried out; done.
- 65 *office:* duty; job.
- 70 *wilt:* the form of 'will' used with 'thou'. (O)
- 70 *credit:* believe.
- 71 *regulation:* ability to regulate; ability to control.
- 75 *dog-star:* a name for one of the stars.
- 76 *crab:* a name for one of the constellations.
- 80 *dividend:* share.
- 97 *confer . . . upon:* give . . . to.
- 112 *long:* for a long time. (O)
- 140 *advantaged:* benefited. (O)

145 *canst:* the form of 'can' used with 'thou'. (O)
147 *become:* be right for. (O)
163 *contracted:* caught; got.

QUESTIONS

1 Explain the following phrases:
   a 'to hear his deductions and enjoy his discoveries' (lines 12–13).
   b 'who find the images of other things stealing away' (lines 16–17).
   c 'the practice of virtue is commanded' (line 35).
   d 'a man who longed to speak what he was yet resolved to suppress' (lines 50–1).
   e 'the hour of imbecility and pain' (line 66).
   f 'made to the different nations of the earth an impartial dividend of rain and sunshine' (lines 79–81).
   g 'the weariness of unremitted vigilance' (lines 92–3).
   h 'I . . . shall not attempt to gain credit by disputation' (lines 122–3).
   i 'The memory of mischief is no desirable fame' (line 146).
   j 'the uncertain continuance of reason' (lines 159–60).

2 Imlac says that the prince should meet some men who have 'grown old in the company of themselves' (line 8). What does he mean by this? How do we know, from what he tells us, that the astronomer is one of these men?
3 Why was the astronomer glad to meet Imlac?
4 Why did the astronomer divert the conversation to another topic when he was praised?
5 Why did Imlac first think that the astronomer had some painful secret?
6 Say briefly what this secret was.
7 Why did it make the astronomer so unhappy?
8 What proof, if any, does the astronomer give of the powers that he thinks he has?
9 Although the astronomer is mad, he is nevertheless exceptionally knowledgeable and virtuous, as Imlac says in lines 157–8. How, in the circumstances, do his knowledge and virtue add to his misery?
10 What similarities can you see between this passage and the extract from Johnson's *Lives of the Poets* (Passage No. 24)?

30 One Disadvantage of Having Money

Charles Lamb (1775-1834) was a Londoner who in the early nineteenth century developed a new way of writing sentimentally and charmingly about everyday life. He is most famous for the essays he contributed to the *London Magazine*, which were signed not with his own name but with the name 'Elia'. They were published later in book form under the titles *The Essays of Elia* and *The Last Essays of Elia*. These extracts from the essay 'Old China' are about a conversation between the writer and his cousin Bridget. It is probably based very closely on a similar conversation between Lamb and his sister, with whom he lived for nearly all of his adult life. It certainly reflects Lamb's own interests: for instance, Lamb was very interested in the Elizabethan dramatists (writers of plays) and the 'folio Beaumont and Fletcher' mentioned here is an early edition of the plays written by a pair of Elizabethan dramatists, Francis Beaumont and John Fletcher, whose work delighted Lamb.

I was talking to my cousin last evening about a set of extraordinary old blue china which we were now for the first time using; and could not help remarking how favourable circumstances had been to us of late years, that we could afford to please the eye sometimes with trifles of this sort—when a passing sentiment seemed to overshade the brows of my companion. I am quick at detecting these summer clouds in Bridget.

'I wish the good old times would come again,' she said, 'when we were not quite so rich. I do not mean that I want to be poor; but there was a middle state'—so she was pleased to ramble on—'in which I am sure we were a great deal happier. A purchase is but a purchase, now that you have money enough and to spare. Formerly it used to be a triumph. When we coveted a cheap luxury (and O! how much ado I had to get you to consent in those times!) we were used to have a debate two or three days before, and to weigh the *for* and *against*, and think what we might spare it out of, and what saving we could hit upon that should be an equivalent. A thing was worth buying then, when we felt the money that we paid for it.

'Do you remember the brown suit, which you made to hang upon you, till all your friends cried shame upon you, it grew so threadbare—

and all because of that folio Beaumont and Fletcher, which you dragged home late at night from Barker's in Covent Garden? Do you remember how we eyed it for weeks before we could make up our minds to the purchase, and had not come to a determination till it was near ten o'clock of the Saturday night, when you set off from Islington, fearing you should be too late—and when the old bookseller with some grumbling opened his shop, and by the twinkling taper (for he was setting bedwards) lighted out the relic from his dusty treasures—and when you lugged it home, wishing it were twice as cumbersome—and when you presented it to me—and when we were exploring the perfectness of it (*collating* you called it)—and while I was repairing some of the loose leaves with paste, which your impatience would not suffer to be left till day-break—was there no pleasure in being a poor man? or can those neat black clothes which you wear now, and are so careful to keep brushed, since we have become rich and finical, give you half the honest vanity, with which you flaunted it about in that over-worn suit—your old corbeau—for four or five weeks longer than you should have done, to pacify your conscience for the mighty sum of fifteen—or sixteen shillings was it?—a great affair we thought it then—which you had lavished on the old folio? Now you can afford to buy any book that pleases you, but I do not see that you ever bring me home any nice old purchases now.

'There was pleasure in eating strawberries, before they became quite common—in the first dish of peas, while they were yet dear—to have them for a nice supper, a treat. What treat can we have now? If we were to treat ourselves now—that is, to have dainties a little above our means, it would be selfish and wicked. It is the very little more that we allow ourselves beyond what the actual poor can get at, that makes what I call a treat—when two people living together, as we have done, now and then indulge themselves in a cheap luxury, which both like; while each apologises, and is willing to take both halves of the blame to his single share. I see no harm in people making much of themselves in that sense of the word. It may give them a hint how to make much of others. But now—what I mean by the word—we never do make much of ourselves. None but the poor can do it. I do not mean the veriest poor of all, but persons as we were, just above poverty.

'I know what you were going to say, that it is mighty pleasant at the end of the year to make all meet—and much ado we used to have every Thirty-first Night of December to account for our exceedings—

many a long face did you make over your puzzled accounts, and in contriving to make it out how we had spent so much—or that we had not spent so much—or that it was impossible we should spend so much next year—and still we found our slender capital decreasing—but then, betwixt ways, and projects, and compromises of one sort or another, and talk of curtailing this charge, and doing without that for the future—and the hope that youth brings, and laughing spirits (in which you were never poor till now) we pocketed up our loss, and in conclusion, with "lusty brimmers" we used to welcome in the "coming guest". Now we have no reckoning at all at the end of the old year—no flattering promises about the new year doing better for us.'

CHARLES LAMB

NOTES

5 *overshade:* cloud; cast a shadow over.
6 *summer clouds:* temporary, not very serious sorrows.
10 *ramble on:* go on talking, without keeping closely to the subject.
12 *and to spare:* and more than enough; and some left over.
15 *weigh the for and against:* carefully consider the arguments in favour and those against.
16 *hit upon:* find by chance; find by a process of trial and error.
19 *made to hang:* kept hanging.
20 *cried shame upon you:* said that you ought to be ashamed of yourself.
25 *set off:* started.
28 *setting bedwards:* on his way to bed. (O)
31 *perfectness:* perfection. (O)
33 *suffer:* allow.
37 *it about:* about.
37 *over-worn:* too worn; too much worn.
37 *corbeau:* dark green, almost black suit.
39 *mighty:* great. Bridget is joking.
44 *yet:* still.
45 *a treat:* something nice which one does not often have, and which is therefore a special pleasure.
46 *above our means:* which cost more than we can really afford.
52 *making much of themselves:* treating themselves generously.
56 *veriest poor:* truly poorest. (O)
59 *make all meet:* balance one's accounts; make one's income balance one's expenses.

60 *exceedings:* overspending. (O)
61 *long:* unhappy.
61 *puzzled:* confused.
62 *make it out:* discover; find out.
64 *slender:* small.
69 *lusty brimmers:* big cups filled to the top (brim).

QUESTIONS

1 What did Bridget mean when she said 'A purchase is but a purchase, now that you have money enough and to spare. Formerly it used to be a triumph' (lines 11–13)?
2 Why did the writer go out to buy the folio Beaumont and Fletcher so late at night?
3 Why did he wish the book were 'twice as cumbersome'?
4 Why, according to Bridget, is it only possible for people 'just above poverty' to have a treat?
5 Why, in the past, did Bridget and the writer always welcome the new year? Why are things different now at the end of the year?

Word Lists

Each list shows the words in the passage that are outside the 3,275 headword vocabulary. The number of the passage is given on the left and the line references follow the words.

1. bedchamber 5
   apprehend 6
   even 9
   undertake 12
   conjecture 18
   intreat 20
   waggoner 22
   brim 23
   quarters 30
   metropolis 30
   readiness 31
   divert 31

   Colossus 32
   asunder 32
   patron 34
   pike 37
   petition 38
   provocation 41
   versed 45
   morose 45
   complexion 45
   comply 46
   dominion 55

   extremity 56
   monarch 57
   fruitful 60
   sublime 61
   celestial 62
   oath 63
   presume 67
   trample 74
   computation 90
   pace 90
   access 94

2. grandpa, *title*
   lariat 2
   serpent 2
   runaway 2
   cactus 3
   gee-up 4
   whoa 4
   creak 8
   flap 10

   tiptoe 17
   candlestick 19
   thump 19
   megaphone 21
   counterpane 24
   bedside 25
   flannel 25
   walnut 26
   smoulder 27

   whisker 27
   hayrick 28
   muffle 30
   quilt 32
   sly 37
   nightmare 37
   fumble 43
   tinkle 43
   sovereign 44

3. gutter 9
   gurgle 9
   pavement 11
   resolute 19

   rout 22
   unstoppable 25
   dizzy 33

   shin 37
   puddle 39
   regain 40

4. fleeting 6

   entrance (*v.*) 21

   thy 24

5. sermon, *title*
   multitude 1
   disciple 2
   meek 6
   righteousness 7
   peacemaker 11
   persecute 13
   revile 15
   prophet 18

   savour 19
   wherewith 20
   thenceforth 20
   bushel 24
   candlestick 25
   glorify 27
   whosoever 30
   smite 30
   thee 31

   thy 31
   sue 32
   twain 34
   thine 38
   despiteful 40
   publican 46
   brethren 47
   moth 51
   mammon 64

raiment 68
behold 69
cubit 72
stature 73
array 77
wherewithal 82
Gentile 83
morrow 87
thereof 89
mete 92
mote 93

hypocrite 97
swine 100
lest 100
trample 100
rend 101
serpent 108
whatsoever 112
strait 114
thereat 116
inward 120

ravening 120
fig 122
thistle 122
hew 127
wherefore 129
prophesy 133
profess 136
iniquity 137
liken 139
scribe 151

6 ham 4
tricycle 6
befall 10
foible 15
inauspicious 17

shin 26
calf 26
detest 28
hi 29
dainty 38

morsel 38
slink 39
reluctant 39
snarl 40

7 thou 1
nay 2

thee 3

thy 10

8 boarding house, *title*
foreman 3
plunder 5
till (*n.*) 5
headlong 5
cleaver 9
enlist 13
sheriff 14
shabby 14
stoop 14
drunkard 14
bailiff 17
imposing 20
artiste 22
music hall 22
stout 27
chummy 29
obscenity 32
comic 36
reunion 37
waltz 38
polka 39
vamp 39
sham 42
slim 44
perverse 47

madonna 47
factor 48
disreputable 49
flirt 54
shrewd 55
complicity 63
perturb 66
balloon (*v.*) 72
sash 73
belfry 73
peal 74
traverse 74
demeanour 76
gloved 76
streak 78
morsel 79
bacon 79
rind 79
pudding 82
reconstruct 84
somewhat 87
connive 89
allusion 90
divine (*v.*) 92
gilt 94
mantelpiece 95

reverie 95
outrage 100
hospitality 102
inexperience 106
reparation 108
brunt 110
rakish 117
publicity 120
lodger 120
whereas 124
pier-glass 127
florid 128
desist 133
fringe 133
recollection 136
acute 137
ridiculous 138
loophole 139
brazen 141
rasp 145
diligence 148
public-house 150
vulgar 158
agitation 172
bosom 173
celibate 175

WORD LISTS

casual 175
caress 176
timid 177
relight 178
gust 179
flannel 180
instep 180
tumbler 188
punch 188
tiptoe 190

clash, *title*
decorous 7
convention 7
riotous 8
caste 9
prestige 11
embarrassment 17
cat-call 18
slam 18
folder 18
signatory 26
founder 27
precede 29

archipelago, *introd.*
disagreeable 3
cannibal 6
pack-horse 6
horrid 8
brute 8
buffalo 8
halter 11
tether (*n.*) 11
helter-skelter 12
demon 12
pathway 14

mamma 4
bachelor 6
tart 7
enamel 7
Lieutenant-
    Governor 9
Viceroy 9
departmental 15

reluctant 191
delirium 193
missus 199
parlour 199
long (*v.*) 205
implacable 208
discomfiture 209
pantry 210
bulldog 212

rowdy 31
heavy-weight 34
boxing 34
runner-up 35
middle-weight 35
raffle 45
flannel 47
slit 47
arm-in-arm 48
stalk (*v.*) 53
choir 54
surplice 54
sneak 55

catastrophe 16
tether (*v.*) 18
ogre 25
lofty 26
somewhat 26
elm 27
scaly 27
bark 27
spine 29
rind 31
pulp 33
eatable 33

gorilla 17
providence 19
avarice 23
era 29
croquet 31
archery 32
revive 32
archer 38

blond 216
profile 226
readjust 226
amiable 229
nape 229
perturbation 231
intricate 234
banister 238
mamma 240

giggle 57
foolhardiness 58
swagger 59
aisle 61
carnation 63
lapel 63
horrify 63
talkative 73
chafe 80
scoff 81
weak-kneed 81
breach 83
disciplinary 84

consistency 34
custard 35
almond 35
intermingle 36
waft 36
sherry 37
incongruity 37
nausea 39
moralist 46
Brazil-nut 49
partial 53
exclusive 55

uplifted 41
phenomenal 45
adorn 45
grotesque 46
ape 47
dragoon 49
stately 53
woo 53

pious 57
precedence 58
irreverent 60
matrimony 61
tournament 65
sumptuous 66
deodar 72
grand-stand 72

gorgeous 80
hideous 80
condescend 82
befit 82
potential 83
tedious 85
string (v.) 92
prompt (v.) 95

imperceptible 98
deliberation 101
nicety 102
mottled 122
shrill 122
jerk 126
snap 128

12 O 1
    ay 1
    nay 14
    bestow 16

mortify 17
commendation 18
commend 21
unseen 31

incessant 37
rotation 38
fiction 41

13 lumpish 4
    pedant 5
    whilst 18

jest 20
elf 27

stupendous 32
lofty 34

14 aphorism, *title*
    endowment 1
    hinder (a.) 14
    sparingly 17
    gluttonous 18

perpetual 21
soothe 30
vale 33
infirmity 33
hazardous 37

conjecture 37
countess 38
dowager 38
confute 44
defensive 46

15 nightingale, *title*
    streamlet 4
    maidenhair 4
    pipe (v.) 4
    wanness 5
    hello 6
    thicket 11
    inconsiderate 16

obstreperous 16
jaunty 16
ode 18
drowsy 18
numbness 19
silvery 20
mediaeval 24
peacock 26

undiluted 31
recall 33
unforlorn 34
straightway 35
toll 37
thee 37
cherubim 40
discrepancy 41

16 scandal, *title*
    gall 8
    honeymoon 8
    dissipation 11
    gala 11
    extravagant 12
    foppery 12
    sneer 14
    dissipate 16
    vexation 22
    nay 25
    uneasiness 26
    notwithstanding 28
    aye 34

perverseness 36
insert 39
feign 40
whence 41
intrigue 43
ladyship 44
disinherit 52
elopement 52
tête-à-tête 55
gross 58
tint 61
mellowness 61
hypocrite 68
envenom 70

slander 71
accountable 79
disagreeable 81
thwart 81
elegant 81
presume 95
tenacious 100
vengeance 101
hurdle 103
utterer 104
forge 104
coiner 104
clipper 105
restrain 106

WORD LISTS 131

malice 110
ye 116

17 indulgent 1
exempt 1
epidemic 2
famine 4
desolation 4
bosom 5
impregnate 6
gale 6
court (v.) 7
husbandman 7
afflict 11
pestilence 11
ravage 13

18 drunkenness, *title*
harp 2
highness 4
wassail 6
virtual 6
superintendence 6
jovial 7
chorus 7
goblet 10
perpendicularity 21
accomplish 21
inflexibility 23
oscillate 24
pendulum 24
requisite 25
rigidity 25
dissipate 26
dizzy 28
wield 28
relax 29
plummet 30
gesticulation 31
footstool 35
eloquence 37
inmate 45
gastronomy 52
groom 53
pantry 53
vigorous 55
dizziness 57

expostulation 118
contempt 120

pestilential 13
malady 15
appellation 16
calamity 18
comet 20
fiery 21
consternation 22
malignity 24
mastiff 28
shudder 32
congeal 33
frightful 33
hideous 35

somewhat 58
impaired 58
dilate 59
whereby 59
feverishness 60
parching 60
impede 61
token 62
fealty 63
cupbearer 65
embankment 67
sturdy 73
gainsay 73
mar 78
stonework 79
sap 79
dislocate 80
floodgate 80
sluice 80
leaky 80
creaky 81
perverse 86
venerable 87
antiquity 87
unamiable 87
indulge 88
innovation 93
equinoctial 93
clash 94

plague 124

draught 38
uneasy 42
tidings 43
dismal 51
smother 54
slaver 56
devour 56
credulous 57
brindled 63
hind 65
frenzy 75
symptom 75
deplore 76

spatter 94
batter 94
presumptuous 95
conclusive 100
approbation 101
material (a.) 108
vindication 135
bard 136
riotous 142
vehement 151
volition 153
dexterous 153
discourse 154
prostrate 155
simultaneous 156
zealous 157
foremost 157
vehemence 158
hurl 158
overthrow 160
rivulet 160
gurgle 160
redeem 161
participate 163
discomfiture 163
skull 164
equilibrium 165
progression 167
jostle 168

19 cavern 2
    novice 3
    prophecy 5
    prophesy 6
    drunken 7
    oracle 8
    discredit 8
    tortuous 10
    pitch-dark 11
    bat 11
    stammer 12
    elocution 13
    unpremeditated 15
    grope 18
    ape 19
    unblinking 21
    toothless 22
    salutation 24

    prop 27
    predecessor 28
    propitiatory 30
    grimace 30
    ivory 35
    extricate 38
    mimic 40
    prophetic 44
    swish 46
    Punic 48
    strangle 49
    sicken 50
    maggot 52
    fawn (v.) 58
    cluck 59
    dribble 60
    obeisance 65
    sprawl 66

    headlong 66
    tremendous 68
    diviner 69
    regularize 71
    interpret 71
    massacre 78
    sloth 82
    effeminacy 83
    un-Roman 83
    injunction 88
    preservative 89
    fluid 89
    casket 89
    posterity 90
    interpretation 91
    shuffle 93
    guarded 94

20 topsy-turvy, *title*
    countryman 3
    sentence (v.) 4
    subdivision 5
    misdemeanour 6
    hitherto 8
    fine (n.) 9
    imprisonment 9
    default 9
    forge 10
    fit (n.) 14
    solicitude 16
    symptom 17
    unreserve 18
    deplorable 19
    pre-natal 22
    post-natal 22
    surpassingly 24
    standpoint 27
    Stock Exchange 31
    amass 32
    justifiable 33
    permissible 34
    fraudulent 35
    pooh-pooh 38
    ailment 38

    practitioner 46
    impair 49
    eminent 50
    reassure 50
    diagnosis 51
    amiss 54
    maternal 54
    consummate 55
    scoundrel 56
    flagitious 57
    homeopathy 60
    allopathy 60
    prescription 62
    embezzle 64
    flogging 65
    prosecute 68
    misplace 68
    sanitary 73
    rigorous 74
    subsequent 78
    competent 79
    semblance 81
    bilious 83
    gross 84
    breach 84
    etiquette 85

    evasive 89
    hardihood 95
    outbreak 96
    ill-humour 96
    extravagant 96
    indisposition 97
    caller 104
    indisposed 113
    afflict 119
    venial 120
    indulgence 122
    catarrh 125
    lenient 126
    indiscretion 128
    atone 129
    bearings 134
    fast (n.) 136
    martyr 144
    gluttony 144
    excursion 146
    incumbent 147
    unalloyed 148
    indulge 149
    pseudo- 154
    industrious 157
    apprentice 158

1 thee, *title*
   thy 7
   chide 22

2 venerable, *introd.*
   salvation 3
   thither 6
   countenance 8
   islander 12
   paganism 13
   pagan 13
   void 17

3 frantic 5
   logic 13
   jest 18
   spiteful 19
   veracious 21

4 idolater 1
   childbed 7
   earl 13
   court (*v.*) 13
   appellation 14
   imply 15
   spiritless 15

5 Academy, *introd.*
   nay 1
   unwieldy 4
   corpulency 5
   grotesque 6
   convulsive 6
   ridiculous 13
   idiot 14
   babe 18
   eccentric 19
   oddity 21
   caricature 22
   facial 22
   contortion 22
   articulate 23
   ruminate 24
   cud 25
   cluck 27
   protrude 27
   vociferation 32

changeful 22
ere 28
sacrament 29

angelic 19
co- 20
allude 25
Hallelujah 26
creator 26
apostolical 27
see (*n.*) 27

sneer 25
bliss 26
champagne 36
dowager 39
malice 39

good-nature 16
esteem 16
sublime 19
predominating 19
lofty 20
imperious 20

uncouthness 34
idol 35
tavern 37
gloomy 37
surly 38
indifferent 38
gloom 39
vile 41
melancholy 41
prodigious 44
repulsive 46
uncouth 46
irascible 47
bully 47
slovenly 47
morbid 48
torment 49
insanity 49
portrait 50
misanthropist 50

farewell 33
lo 33

pope 28
entreat 28
undertake 31
renowned 35
exhortation 37
insert 39
ecclesiastical 40

hideous 41
toucan 46
horrid 52
P.S. 57

inflame 22
high-born 23
dame 23
solace 26
bestow 40
sally 40

doom (*v.*) 50
counterbalance 52
repellent 53
enchanting 55
churlishness 55
dictatorial 56
flout 57
courteous 58
ill-mannered 58
playful 59
morbidity 59
solitude 63
biography 68
vocation 74
slothful 75
customary 78
livelihood 79
reproach 79
indolence 79
flaw 80

commend 81
denunciation 84
idler 85

assiduous 87
conversationalist 91

conventional 94
studious 95

26 ply 4
stitch 5
dolorous 7
pitch 7
aloof 10
barbarous 14
seam 21
gusset 21

shroud 32
phantom 34
grisly 34
fast (n.) 38
flag (v.) 42
shatter 45
chime 50
benumb 55

eaves 61
brood 62
swallow (n.) 62
twit 64
cowslip 66
primrose 66
respite 74
briny 78

27 alight 1
anoint 3
propensity 5
foible 8
parson 9
bestride 10
dexterity 12
pace 13
disengage 16
contusion 17
camphorated 19
likewise 22
surly 22
footman 25
chafe 30
damn 31
stride 35

snap 36
excommunicate 37
farthing 37
dialogue 38
gush 46
outdo 47
courtesy 47
nostril 49
assail 50
antagonist 50
sprawl 51
bloody 53
lo 55
hog 55
dresser 56
countenance 59
trickle 59

thence 59
garment 60
gentlewoman 63
impetuosity 65
hearty 67
cuff 67
knack 68
whilst 72
dexterous 73
horrid 77
combatant 79
posture 79
fray 80
vengeance 81
apprehension 87
pudding 88
intermeddle 89

28 siren 4
drone 6
incredible 7
fuchsia 8
zinnea 8
recollection 10
straddle 15
searchlight 16
terminate 16
swab 16
suburban 17

thump 17
boom 17
embarrass 20
lengthy 21
whatsoever 27
fatalism 27
shutter 29
heave 35
satin 35
clumsy 36
tadpole 37

minnow 37
lash 39
crate 43
siding 44
multiple 46
threshold 55
coruscate 56
traverse 57
countless 58
transfiguration 61
texture 64

29 solitude 5
hazard 7
converse 7
observatory 8

astronomer 9
unwearied 10
celestial 11
deduction 13

fluent 14
relax 21
desirous 24
profundity 26

capacious 27
retentive 28
discourse 28
integrity 29
benevolence 29
contemplation 35
enamoured 38
sublime 38
haughtiness 39
courteous 39
communicative 39
ostentation 40
indifference 43
divert 44
long (v.) 51
suppress 51
vehement 52
injunction 52
turret 57
satellite 58
Jupiter 58
tempest 58
awhile 59
thy 61
requisite 64
fortitude 64

imbecility 66
devolve 66
thee 67
testimony 68
conduce 69
likewise 69
thou 70
tropic 73
restrain 75
mitigate 75
fervour 75
elemental 76
hitherto 76
multitude 77
equinoctial 77
impartial 80
obscurity 84
token 85
impart 89
deem 89
unremitted 92
vigilance 93
dominion 99
second (v.) 100
wither 103
inundation 107

concurrence 109
disputation 123
infirmity 125
regulator 126
successor 127
diligent 136
innumerable 137
ecliptic 139
disposition 139
imaginable 141
solar 142
unacquainted 142
indulge 143
innovation 144
renowned 145
inflexible 150
bequeath 153
narration 154
convulse 155
affliction 156
calamity 158
continuance 160
recollect 161
abash 161
malady 163

brow 5
covet 13
O 13
ado 13
threadbare 20
folio 21
eye (v.) 23
grumble 27
relic 28

lug 29
cumbersome 30
collate 31
day-break 33
finical 36
flaunt 36
pacify 38
lavish 40

strawberry 43
dainty 46
indulge 50
contrive 62
betwixt 65
compromise 65
curtail 66
pocket (v.) 68